REDWOOD
NATIONAL & STATE PARKS

A wonderfully accessible little guide that not only describes all kinds
of short, manageable walks, it also gives the history of each area.
—North Coast Journal

REDWOOD
NATIONAL & STATE PARKS

JERRY & GISELA ROHDE

THE MOUNTAINEERS BOOKS

THE MOUNTAINEERS BOOKS
is the nonprofit publishing arm of The Mountaineers, an organization founded in 1906 and dedicated to the exploration, preservation, and enjoyment of outdoor and wilderness areas.

1001 SW Klickitat Way, Suite 201, Seattle, WA 98134

First edition: first printing 2004, second printing 2009, third printing 2011, fourth printing 2015, fifth printing 2018

Manufactured in the United States of America

Acquiring Editor: Christine U. Hosler
Project Editor: Laura Drury
Copy Editor: Colin Chisholm
Cover and Book Design: The Mountaineers Books
Layout: Mayumi Thompson
Cartographer: Moore Creative Designs, Profiles: Judy Petry
All photographs by the authors unless otherwise noted.

Cover photograph: James Martin
Frontispiece: *Avenue of the Giants near High Rock*

Library of Congress Cataloging-in-Publication Data
Rohde, Jerry.
  Best short hikes in Redwood National and State parks / Jerry and Gisela Rohde.—1st ed.
    p. cm.
  ISBN 0-89886-716-9
  1. Hiking—California, Northern—Guidebooks. 2. Hiking—California—Redwood National Park—Guidebooks. 3. California, Northern—Guidebooks. 4. Redwood National Park (Calif.)—Guidebooks. I. Rohde, Gisela. II. Title.
  GV199.42.C2R64 2004
  917.94—dc22

                              2004018038

ISBN (paperback): 978-0-89886-716-9
ISBN (ebook): 978-1-59485-147-6

CONTENTS

DEL NORTE COAST REDWOODS STATE PARK

JEDEDIAH SMITH REDWOODS STATE PARK

MAP KEY

▬▬▬▬▬	Paved Road	(101)	US Highway
════════	Unpaved Road	Δ	Campground
▪▪▪▪▪▪▪▪▪	Main Trail	ΔH	Hike-in Campground
··············	Other Trail	🎋	Picnic Area
～～～	River/Creek	🏠	Visitor Center
～～～	River/Ocean	🏠 E	Entrance Station
⟰	Waterfall	≍	Year-round Bridge
❹	Hike Number	≍ S	Summer Bridge
Ⓟ	Trailhead Parking	●━●	Locked Gate
⟶	Direction Arrow	■	Point of interest

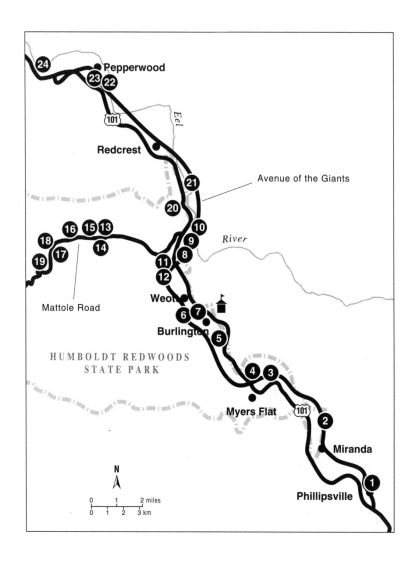

Pepperwood

101

Redcrest

Avenue of the Giants

Eel

River

Mattole Road

Weott

Burlington

HUMBOLDT REDWOODS
STATE PARK

Myers Flat

101

Miranda

Phillipsville

N

0   1   2 miles
0 1 2 3 km

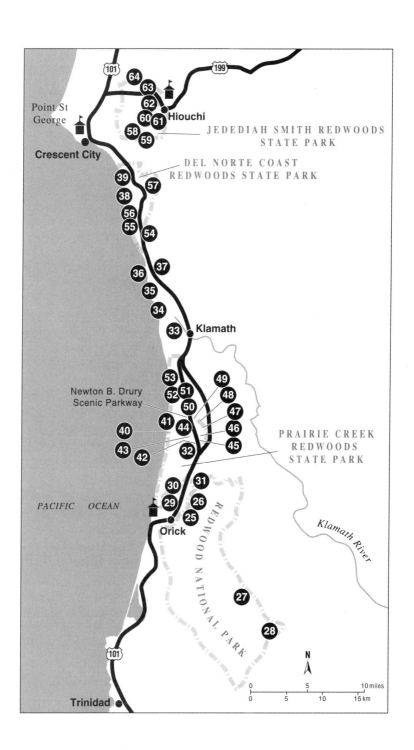

101

199

64

63

62

60 61 **Hiouchi**

Point St George

58

59

JEDEDIAH SMITH REDWOODS STATE PARK

Crescent City

DEL NORTE COAST REDWOODS STATE PARK

39

57

38

56

55

54

36 37

35

34

33 **Klamath**

53

49

Newton B. Drury Scenic Parkway

52 51

48

50

47

41

40

44

46

43

42

32

45

PRAIRIE CREEK REDWOODS STATE PARK

30 31

PACIFIC OCEAN

29 26

25

Orick

R E D W O O D

N A T I O N A L

P A R K

Klamath River

27

28

N

101

0   5   10 miles
0   5   10   15 km

Trinidad

A QUICK GUIDE TO THE HIKES

Hiking in a hurry? Want to cut to the chase when choosing a hike? The handy "quick guide" chart, below, will help. The hikes are grouped by their single most important feature, with a summary of additional important information. Selecting a hike with this system is as easy as one, two, three: 1) Just glance over the categories until you find the one you want, 2) refer to any of the hike descriptions listed in that category that seem of interest, and 3) make your choice. Happy trails!

HIKE	MILES	DIFFICULTY	OTHER FEATURES
Hikes in Old-Growth Redwoods			
9. Mahan Plaque	0.6	easy	historical marker, wildflowers
10. Founders Grove	0.5	easy	noteworthy tree, wildflowers
11. Rockefeller	0.65	easy	historical marker, river
14. Bull Creek Flats	3.55	moderate	noteworthy tree, creek
20. The Five Allens	2.8	strenuous	waterfall, mixed forest
22. French Grove	0.75	easy	wildflowers, noteworthy tree
23. Drury-Chaney Groves	2.45	moderate	mixed forest, historic road
26. Lady Bird Johnson	1.3	easy	plants, historic road
30. Trillium Falls	3.15	moderate	elk herd, waterfall
43. James Irvine–Miner's Ridge	7.6	strenuous	historic trail, mixed forest
46. Cathedral Trees–Big Tree	2.6	moderate	historic marker, noteworthy trees
47. Trail-Through Trees	0.8	moderate	wildflowers, historic road
51. Hope Creek–Ten Taypo	3.75	strenuous	creek, mixed forest
58. Boy Scout Tree	5.6	strenuous	noteworthy tree, waterfall
Hikes with Beaches and/or Coast			
34. Mouth of Klamath Overlook	1.1	strenuous	mouth of Klamath River
35. Hidden Beach	6.2	strenuous	wildflowers, mixed forest, Pacific Ocean
36. Yurok	1.15	easy	pond, wildflowers, coastal scenery

HIKE	MILES	DIFFICULTY	OTHER FEATURES
Hikes with Beaches and/or Coast (continued)			
38. Nickel Creek– Enderts Beach	2	moderate	historic highway, wildflowers
39. Crescent Beach Overlook	4	moderate	meadow, plants
41. Gold Bluffs– Gold Dust Falls	3	moderate	elk herd, waterfalls
52. Ossagon Rocks	4.8	strenuous	elk herd, alder thickets
53. Crothers Cove	1.8	strenuous	historic site, lagoon
55. Damnation Creek	4.2	strenuous	historic roads, mixed forest
61. Stout Grove	1.6	moderate	river, mixed forest
64. Leiffer-Ellsworth	2.2	moderate	historic road, mixed forest
Hikes with Prairies			
13. Look Prairie	3.2	strenuous	historic homesite, fall color
16. Albee-Thornton	7.9	strenuous	old-growth tanoaks and madrones
17. Whiskey Prairie	3.7	moderate	fall color, scenic views
19. Pole Line Road	4.8	strenuous	wildflowers, scenic views
45. Elk Prairie	2.6	moderate	elk herd, mixed forest
Hikes with Rivers, Creeks, or Ponds			
5. Kent Grove– South Fork Eel	1.2	easy	old-growth redwoods, fall color
12. Decker Creek	2.75	moderate	old-growth redwoods, plants
21. High Rock	1.2	moderate	old-growth redwoods, wildflowers, old wagon road
25. Redwood Creek	3.2	moderate	elk herd, wildflowers
31. Lost Man Creek	0.8	easy	old-growth redwoods, wildflowers
33. Marshall Pond	2	moderate	old-growth redwoods, wildlife
42. Nature	0.9	easy	old-growth redwoods
44. West Ridge– Prairie Creek	6.45	strenuous	old-growth redwoods, scenic views, noted tree
50. Little Creek	0.5	easy	wildflowers, historical marker
57. Trestle-Skyline	3.1	moderate	historic logging site, mixed forest
62. Hiouchi– Smith River	4	moderate	old-growth redwoods, plants, river
Hikes with Lots of Wildflowers or Natural Scenery			
2. Dry Creek	3.55	moderate	creek, plants
3. Sa-bug-gah-nah	1.1	moderate	river, historic highway, wildflowers

Continued on next page

HIKE	MILES	DIFFICULTY	OTHER FEATURES
Hikes with Lots of Wildflowers or Natural Scenery (continued)			
4. Williams Grove–Hidden Springs	5.2	strenuous	view of river, mixed forest
7. Burlington-Gould	2.5	moderate	historical home site, mixed forest
29. Skunk Cabbage Creek	2.8	easy	creek, mixed forest
40. Fern Canyon	1.8	moderate	historic mining site, plants
48. Prairie Creek Rhododendron	2.3	moderate	old-growth redwoods, plants
49. Brown Creek	3.6	moderate	old-growth redwoods, historic grove
54. Del Norte Coast Rhododendron	5.4	strenuous	old-growth redwoods, plants
Hikes with Terrific Fall Color			
59. Mill Creek South	1.4	easy	creek, mixed forest
60. Mill Creek North	5.7	strenuous	old-growth redwoods, creek
63. Simpson-Reed and Peterson	0.8	easy	old-growth redwoods, mixed forest
Hikes with Historical Features			
1. F. K. Lane Grove	0.45	easy	old-growth redwoods, wildflowers
6. Forest Lodge	2	moderate	river, old-growth redwoods
8. Big Cut	2.4	moderate	wildflowers, old-growth redwoods, four fireplaces
15. Addie Johnson Grave	2.3	moderate	old-growth redwoods, plants, pioneer grave
18. Hamilton Barn	1.5	easy	creek, plants
24. Old Highway 101 South	0.6	easy	old-growth redwoods, creek, historic bridge
27. Dolason Prairie	2.6	strenuous	prairie/woodlands, mixed forest, pioneer sheep shed
28. Lyons Ranch	4.65	strenuous	wildflowers, prairie/woodlands, pioneer ranch
32. Wagon Road South	0.6	easy	old-growth redwoods, prairie, historic road
37. Wagon Road North	4.0	moderate	view of coast, mixed forest, historic road
56. Old Highway 101 North	5.1	strenuous	old-growth redwoods, wildflowers, historic road

INTRODUCTION: HIKING IN BIG TREE COUNTRY

Old-timers used to say of the coast redwoods that it took "two men and a boy to see all the way to the top." The trees, as a species, are big to begin with, but on the North Coast they are huge. Photos exist of entire schools of students standing on a single stump, of burly loggers dwarfed by the diameter of a fresh-fallen tree, of sections of logs so thick that they barely fit on the bed of a railroad car. When the National Geographic Society sent an investigator in the 1960s to find the world's tallest tree, it was to Humboldt County that he first came, and it was there he found it—a streamside giant 367.8 feet tall, with three neighbors that were 367.4, 364.3, and 352.3 feet tall. The discovery revitalized the movement to establish a Redwood National Park, which became reality just four years later. It joined three state redwood parks, all dating from the 1920s, that lay along the Highway 101 and Highway 199 corridors in the far northwestern corner of California.

Today those highways, along with nearby scenic alternate routes, make it easy to gain access to dozens of trailheads within the parks. The vast majority of the sixty-four hikes described in this book are located adjacent to paved roadways, while a few require driving on well-maintained gravel roads. Most trails are open year-round, but some require use of summer-only bridges to cross certain creeks or rivers. Others may be closed intermittently during rainy or snowy weather. In addition, some of the routes are best seen at certain times of year—perhaps spring or summer for wildflower displays, or fall for the changing of the leaves.

As you might expect, most of the hikes take you through redwood forests, but some offer additional attractions—grassy meadows, river crossings—and a few take you to completely different environments, such as oak woodlands or ocean beaches. Some trails follow streams or rivers; others are built on historic roads. Some take you to storybook landscapes seen nowhere else on earth, while others take you above the coastal fog or into the depths of fern-filled canyons. Some take you back in time, while others give you hopeful visions of the future. All of the trails will reward you with some special wonder—if you just put on your boots and hike them.

THE COAST REDWOOD

Imagine a 7-foot-tall Christmas tree. Think of how it nearly touches the ceiling in the living room of a typical house. Then imagine that tree grown fifty times taller, fifty times larger, so that it would take a small skyscraper to contain it. The tree you would then be looking at would be an old-growth coast redwood.

Now imagine not one such tree but hundreds of them, acres upon acres of them, filling a canyon 3 miles long and 300 yards wide. Imagine the space within it, where sounds are dampened to near silence, where only the dimmest rays of light penetrate. You are imagining a single stand of coast redwoods.

Lastly, imagine not just one such stand, but dozens of them, linked together in the stream and river canyons, and rising up the hills to cover the nearby ridges. Imagine these stands stretching almost without interruption all the way from southern Oregon to beyond Big Sur on the California coast. You are imagining what was once the coast redwood forest.

Once there were a dozen different species of redwoods, but about a million years ago the Ice Age put an end to nine of them and drastically reduced the ranges of the rest. The coast redwood (*Sequoia sempervirens*) is one of the three that remained. California is also home to its closest cousin, the giant sequoia (*Sequoiadendron giganteum*), which is found at several locations in the Sierra Nevada. The other relative, the dawn redwood (*Metasequoia glyptostroboides*), is not so well known, since it is native only to a remote and rugged section of China.

Coast redwoods are both sturdy *and* vulnerable. Under the right conditions, they can live two thousand years or more, protected by a fire- and insect-resistant bark that grows up to a foot thick and by a supply of tannins and phenolics that render the trees' wood cells difficult to digest. But the huge trees have a weakness—a shallow root system that grows only a few feet deep. Normally this causes little

Opposite: *Watering trough made from redwood log*

difficulty, for the individual redwoods cleverly stretch their roots out laterally and intertwine them with those of their neighbors, lending each other considerable support. Nonetheless, a huge tree in the middle of a grove will occasionally plunge to earth, weakening the root network of its cohorts and perhaps bumping one or more of them on its way down. Some of these nearby trees may then also fall—six, eight, perhaps even more—until a set of half-million-ton pickup sticks is littered about an opening in the forest. Trees at the edge of a stand suffer special risks: they may be undermined by overflowing creeks or rivers, or severe windstorms may deliver knockout punches.

Like most trees, coast redwoods reproduce from their seeds, but they also regenerate from sprouts growing from burl collars that develop near the base of the trees' trunks. Redwoods rise on straight shafts that are often limbless, on mature trees, for a hundred feet and more. Many adult redwoods develop what are called reiterated trunks—offshoots that sprout from an injured area and then grow upward parallel to main stem, or bole, of the tree. The trunk itself

Huge burls at base of redwood, Simpson-Reed Loop

contains a marvelous hydraulic system, capable of pumping hundreds of gallons of moisture upward in a single day, where it is transpired into the surrounding air. With such a high demand for water, redwoods require the particular climate of the wet, temperate northern California coast to survive. The canopy of an old-growth redwood forest contains its own unique environment, one that rope-climbing researchers are just beginning to explore. Here they have found various species of wildlife and plants living in a specialized, high-rise habitat a hundred feet and more above the forest floor. The wonders of the coast redwood continue to reveal themselves in the new millennium, making *Sequoia sempervirens* truly a tree for the ages.

THE "WONDER" WOOD

Redwoods have long been esteemed not just for their majesty and beauty, but also for their utility. For centuries, coastal Indian tribes used redwood for their canoes, as roof and wall planks for their houses, and for tools and other implements. Spanish colonizers hewed what they called the *palo colorado* into roof beams for the Santa Clara and San Francisco missions, and Father Junipero Serra, the founder of California's chain of missions, was buried in a coffin made of redwood. Russian fur traders constructed fifty-nine buildings out of redwood at Fort Ross, their Sonoma Coast outpost. Much of early day San Francisco was built of redwoods cut from the hills surrounding the bay. All of this was but a prelude to the heyday of redwood use, which was launched by an advertising campaign that eventually caused the tree's timber to be known as the "wonder" wood. Over the decades the uses of *Sequoia sempervirens* were chronicled in a superlative set of testimonials that included the following:

▪ In 1874 the Santa Rosa Baptist Church was built from the timber of a single redwood tree.

▪ When asked to create the "most magnificently appointed train in the world," George Pullman selected redwood for the inside finish of the coaches.

▪ Because so many redwood buildings emerged unscathed by the fire that followed the 1906 San Francisco earthquake, the mayor's emergency building committee directed that all new structures be made of either galvanized iron or redwood.

▪ Redwood was shipped to both the Argentine Republic and the East Indian Islands, where it remained untouched by the voracious red ants that ate all other woods.

- Two Massachusetts piano makers required redwood for their piano cases, as it "made the most perfect sounding boards...[that]...would not warp, twist, or crack."
- The king of Denmark was sent a folding redwood bedstead by a San Francisco bank. It was placed in His Majesty's sleeping compartment for his "personal" use.
- By the 1940s, sports fields across the continent contained seats made from redwood, including the football stadiums at Stanford, Pittsburgh, Michigan, Iowa, Virginia, Louisiana, and McGill Universities, and also Fenway and Comiskey baseball parks.
- The San Francisco–Oakland Bay Bridge used over seven million board feet of redwood lumber, including more than 105,000 ties selected especially for their durability and high insulating value.

In addition, hundreds of smaller bridges were constructed out of rot-resistant redwood, along with countless pipelines, guard rails, posts, trestles, wharf piles, piers, grape stakes, silos, flood gates, feeders, water and septic tanks, irrigation flumes, wine vats, and cigar boxes.

It took a while, but in time all of those wharf piles, wine vats, and cigar boxes started to add up, and people gradually began to look at the vanishing redwood forest and wonder if soon there would be any "wonder" wood left. The answer invigorated a movement that has continued to this day.

SAVING THE REDWOODS

If the United States Congress had acted decisively, the country could have had a national redwood park more than a century earlier than it did. But federal politicians dithered while loggers felled acre after acre of the "big sticks," and it was left to the Save-the-Redwoods League and the State of California to ride to the rescue, acquiring tracts of forestland in key locations and developing them into a series of magnificent state parks.

It was not for lack of trying that the idea of a national redwood park languished among the legislators. A member of the California Assembly proposed federal protection of redwoods in 1852, and the secretary of the interior, Carl Schurtz, made a similar suggestion in 1879. President Theodore Roosevelt endorsed a redwood park in 1904 and still nothing happened. Four years later came a most remarkable request: 1400 schoolchildren from Eureka, which must have meant nearly all of the city's students, petitioned the United States government to "ask for the establishment of a Redwood national park." Still no action, nor did

Old tractor hauling logs

any of three proposals in the early 1910s gain any headway. Meanwhile, workers on the Redwood Highway were pushing south into Eel River country while another crew nearby was busy building a rail line towards San Francisco. With a transportation network nearly completed, loggers could soon invade the rich redwood forests of the South Fork Eel and start shipping the results of their work to San Francisco.

Enter the Save-the-Redwoods League. Alarmed by the first cutting along the South Fork, a group of wealthy and influential preservationists formed the League in 1918 and started raising funds (and public awareness) to help protect the great trees. With the federal government apparently paralyzed, the League joined forces with the State of California, which had already established a redwood park in 1901 at Big Basin, north of Santa Cruz, and soon the North Coast could boast one of its own—some 2200 acres strung out along the Redwood Highway that is now part of Humboldt Redwoods State Park.

The redwoods of Humboldt and Del Norte Counties were, by general agreement, the most impressive in the state. It was thus no surprise that three other North Coast parks soon followed Humboldt Redwoods—Prairie Creek in 1923, Del Norte Coast in 1925, and Jedediah Smith in 1928. What had been called "the world's greatest forest," a huge stand of redwoods on Bull Creek, a tributary of the South Fork Eel, became part of Humboldt Redwoods in 1931. Preservationists could at last breathe a sigh of relief.

But it was to be a short sigh. Soon redwood lovers were gasping at the rapid cutting of unprotected old-growth timberland, which had been accelerated by the advent of gasoline-powered chain saws and powerful mechanized log-moving equipment. While the state, with steady support from the Save-the-Redwoods League, continued to add acreage to its parks, preservationists held out hope that the federal government would act to protect the trees while there were still enough of them left to form a national park.

The catalyst proved to be the discovery, in 1963, of the tallest tree, a 367.8-foot skyscraper that a National Geographic Society naturalist located in a remote section of northern Humboldt County's Redwood Creek. Spurred by the find, which was situated just across the creek from a logging site, Congress finally passed a park bill, and in October 1968 President Lyndon B. Johnson signed the act establishing Redwood National Park. The centerpiece of the new park was an 8000-acre band of old-growth that ran along the hillside above Redwood Creek and included the tall trees area.

But nearby, the timber companies kept cutting, and the erosional runoff from the creek canyon's newly shorn slopes threatened to undermine the tallest tree and several other nearby giants. To protect them, a park expansion bill was approved in 1978 over the heavy opposition of loggers and lumbermen, and Redwood National Park nearly doubled in size. Although much of the newly acquired land had already been cut, the expansion allowed the park to gain control of most of the lower Redwood Creek drainage, thus improving the survival chances for the old-growth trees that remained there.

Even today the parks continue to expand. Humboldt Redwoods has grown to over 53,000 acres, adding to its luster as the largest redwood park in the state. In 2002 the Save-the-Redwoods League acquired 25,000 acres of land, almost all of it logged, in the Mill Creek drainage that will link the Del Norte Coast and Jedediah Smith State Parks. So it is that motorists driving along Highway 101 and Highway 199 through Humboldt and Del Norte counties will pass through or near almost 200,000 acres of redwood parkland—a wide-ranging mix that includes coastal beaches, oak woodland, regenerating cutover forest, and the finest groves of old-growth redwoods that still stand.

It is true that what remains is but a small fraction of the great redwood forest of two hundred years ago, which covered nearly two million acres. But if Theodore Roosevelt, those 1400 Eureka schoolchildren, and the countless others who struggled to save the redwoods

were to visit the parks today and walk beside the shaded waters of
Prairie Creek, or pace beneath the giant trees of Dyerville Flat, or
pause beside the great grove at the mouth of Mill Creek, they would
likely linger until they lost any sense of discontent. For there is a great
power in these trees, whether it be just one of them, or a hundred, or
numbers beyond counting. Anyone who comes into their presence
can feel that power, be changed by it, and come to know that wherever there is an ancient redwood, there is a place that combines the
wonder of the past with the promise of the future, creating a present
that is healing, comforting, and good.

TALL TREE TERMINOLOGY

A select set of words is used when speaking of things in redwood country—logging equipment and activities, the local landscape, and the
trees themselves. Here are definitions of some of the terms you are
most apt to encounter.

albino redwood—sprouts that have grown from the base of a
normal redwood but that lack chlorophyll; they are rare, white
in color, waxy looking, and rely on the host redwood for
sustenance.

alluvium—silts and gravels that wash down rivers and creeks and
collect at various locations. Alluvium is rich in the nutrients
needed by redwoods for growth.

bole—another name for a tree's trunk.

bolt—a section of redwood, several feet long, that was often hewn
by hand into split stuff.

burl—the wartlike outgrowth on a redwood trunk that contains
numerous buds.

butt—the bottom end of a tree, which frequently flares outward in
redwoods; because the butts often contained tough-grained,
heavy wood, and because their flared shape made them much
thicker than the rest of the tree, loggers would often cut the
trunk above the butt while standing on scaffolding.

cathedral trees—a cluster of redwoods, roughly forming a circle,
that have grown up from sprouts at the base of a decayed host tree.

chimney tree—a redwood whose entire interior has been burned
away by fire, leaving a hollow trunk that resembles a chimney.

flat—a level area, usually located along a river or near a creek
mouth, that contains nutrient-rich alluvium; exceptionally large
redwoods often grow there.

goosepen tree—a redwood whose base has been partially burned out by fire, leaving an opening that is large enough to serve as a pen for geese or other farm animals.

spiketop—a redwood whose top has died and lost its foliage due to lack of water.

split stuff—forest products that were hand hewn from bolts of redwood. The bolts from the butt (lower) end of a redwood were tougher and used for ties, while the wood farther up, which split better, was made into grape stakes and fence posts.

springboard—a narrow piece of wood, several feet long, that had one end fitted into a notch cut into the lower part of a redwood. Loggers stood on planks laid across the springboards when cutting a tree some distance above its base.

stobber—a short, thick post, usually about one foot high, often set in rows along park roadsides or parking areas to prevent vehicle encroachment.

tanbarking—the removal of the bark from tanoak trees. The tannin contained in the bark was used by tanneries for curing leather.

widow maker—a large limb that breaks off from a redwood and plunges to earth, often imbedding itself upright in the ground. If it hit a married logger it lived up to its name.

PLANTS AND ANIMALS

The public lands covered in this guidebook are all designated "redwood" parks, after their most prominent attraction. But besides the great trees, there are hundreds of other living things that call the parklands home. Here are some of the redwoods' most notable neighbors:

Plants

Three other large conifers keep the coast redwood company—Douglas-fir, western hemlock, and Sitka spruce. The latter is not found in Humboldt Redwoods State Park, since, except for a few scatterings in Mendocino County, its southern range ends near the town of Ferndale. In the northern parks, however, spruces grow to great size, often out-competing redwoods, which do not like salt air, in coastal locations. Douglas-fir, which sometimes grows almost as tall as redwoods, is more often found on hillslopes than on the rich alluvial benchlands where redwoods excel. Western hemlock, notable for its dense foliage, is the smallest of the four conifers and is usually overtopped by the others in a mixed forest setting.

Frequently joining the conifers are three trees with evergreen leaves. Most common is tanoak, which despite its name is not a true oak, although it does produce an acorn so tasty that it was the favorite of local Indians. California bay, sometimes called laurel or pepperwood, has aromatic leaves that often scent the trailside. In Humboldt Redwoods State Park they are often joined by Pacific madrone, a spectacular tree known for its twisting trunks, picturesquely peeling bark, and bright red autumnal berries.

Deciduous trees mainly fall into two groups. The water lovers, which are found near streams and other wet areas, have leaves

Bigleaf maple in flower

that usually color dramatically in fall. Bigleaf maple, red alder, and various willows are common throughout most low-elevation areas in the parks. Less frequently seen is Oregon ash, noted for its compound leaves, and the largest tree of the group, black cottonwood. Drier, upland locations are usually home to the second set of leaf shedders, the oaks. Both Oregon white oak and California black oak are found in woodland settings, most notably in the Bald Hills of Redwood National Park and on the slopes above Bull Creek in Humboldt Redwoods State Park. Also found at Humboldt Redwoods is canyon live oak, which grows where there are suitably rocky, sunny cliffs—even near the rivers. Pacific dogwood has its own niche, preferring forested areas with a bit of sunlight.

Large shrubs include the delicate California hazel and the colorful vine maple, along with cascara, which is sometimes classified as a small tree. Berry bushes abound in various settings: salal, and both evergreen and red huckleberry prefer the shade of the forest, while thimbleberry, salmonberry, and coast red elderberry like more open and moist areas. Both blueblossom and snowbrush—blue- and white-flowered species of ceanothus, respectively—perfume the air in early summer. Ocean spray and Pacific ninebark both provide

Pacific starflowers

creamy clusters of flowers. Elk clover, found in Humboldt Redwoods, has umbels of small berries that turn deep purple in fall. In the parks to the north, Pacific rhododendron and western azalea flower spectacularly in spring.

Sword fern is found throughout the redwood forest; lady, giant chain, and five-finger ferns favor damp places. Deer fern likes the banks by sides of trails, leather fern perches high in trees or sometimes along their trunks, and licorice fern grows on both trees and rocks.

Flowers in the redwood forest are numerous. Among the most noticeable and noteworthy are redwood sorrel, western trillium, redwood and smooth yellow violet, clintonia, fat and thin false Solomon seal, Hooker's and Smith's fairybell, calypso orchid, fetid adder's tongue, Columbia lily, Siberian candyflower, Pacific windflower, and Pacific starflower. In the oak woodlands areas are giant delphinium, hayfield tarweed, firecracker flower, various lupines, California poppy, and certain clarkias. Irises grow in a variety of locations.

Many other interesting plants lie along the hiking trails and are often noted in the hike descriptions. If you enjoy trying to identify them, take along a specialized guidebook or two and sharpen your plant-sighting skills. It is one of the best ways we know to enrich a hike.

Wildlife

Lots of critters make their homes in the parks, but unlike plants they don't stay in one place for long and are often secretive, which makes them harder to see. One exception is the banana slug, a large, yellowish, shell-less gastropod that creeps so slowly across the forest floor that it seldom avoids detection. At the other end of the spectrum, Roosevelt elk can move quickly (do not ever try to race one), but since they have little to fear from most humans, they usually remain where they are when people come into their vicinity. *Warning: Do not approach elk; they are large, quick, and may attack when threatened. Black bear and mountain lion can also pose threats. Check at park visitor centers for recommended safety practices and for reports of recent sightings.*

Roosevelt elk, which inhabit Prairie Creek Redwoods State Park and the southern sections of Redwood National Park, are the most visible of the parks' mammals, but you might also see black bears, raccoons, skunks, and various squirrels or chipmunks. At Marshall Pond (Hike 33) you may spy beavers or river otters. The most you will probably ever see of a woodrat is its house, but that is quite spectacular— an intricately arranged pile of sticks and debris that can form a dome four feet high.

Raccoon near picnic area

Birds abound in the parks and may be seen or heard in a variety of settings. Along the coast look for cormorants, gulls, and pelicans, while wetlands may display herons and egrets. Streams and rivers often reverberate to the ratcheting rattle of kingfishers, and ospreys may dive from on high in search of prey. Forested areas shelter hermit thrushes, winter wrens, and woodpeckers. Vaux's swifts nest in redwood snags, spotted owls inhabit mixed forest, and ruffed grouses sound in woodlands.

Becoming more familiar with the parks' plants and wildlife can transform hiking from mere exercise into a much richer experience, where you come to know and appreciate the vast array of species that share the surroundings with you. The park visitor centers and local bookstores have many field guides that will help you focus on your particular interest. Among the less expensive but more useful ones are "Finder" series by the Nature Study Guild, and the Peterson Field Guides. There's always a place for one or more of these in any well-equipped day pack. Look in Appendix II for titles.

TAKING TO THE TRAILS

HOW TO USE THIS GUIDEBOOK

As part of the Best Short Hikes series, this book is designed for people of all levels of ability, interest, and experience. We, the authors, have been hiking in the five parks covered here for more than twenty years, and we have selected routes that while "short" (usually taking only a half hour to a half day), are also what we consider the "best," based on our experience. You'll find world-famous trails here, such as those at the Founder's Grove and Fern Canyon, but you'll also learn of little-used gems that are unknown to almost everyone except fanatical park users.

The previous section of the book, "Getting to Know the Parks," provides background information that will enhance your hiking experience. We suggest reading through it before hitting the trails. The subsequent sections briefly describe each of the five redwood parks and the hiking routes we have selected for each of them. The hike descriptions are organized as follows:

Number and name of hike: As closely as possible, the hikes are arranged from south to north within each park, with the parks also presented in the same sequence. Redwood National Park, which is divided into separate units adjacent to the three northern state parks, has all of its hikes listed together but in three subsections—one for each unit. *Note: the names for some hikes are the same as the names of the actual trails. In other cases, the hike names reflect destinations or other features; if so, the names of the trail(s) used for the hike are provided in the text.*

Features: Here we briefly list the most outstanding attractions of the hike. A glance at this section should help you decide if a particular hike is worth further investigation.

Distance: The total (as opposed to one-way) length of the hike. Note that the routes we have selected all return to their starting points, so there is no need to arrange car shuttles or plan complicated connections. Some hikes offer optional longer routes; if so, we alert you to that here and provide detailed information at the end of the hike description.

Elevation gain: The difference between the lowest and highest point of the hike. The elevation profile will indicate if there are additional elevation changes due to rises and drops in the trail.

Difficulty: Our assessment of how hard the trail is for entry-level hikers. We evaluate a combination of distance, elevation gain, and trail condition to arrive at one of three degrees of difficulty: **Easy:** hikes of 1.5 miles or less with little or no elevation gain; suitable for all hikers. **Moderate:** hikes of 1.5 to 4 miles with little elevation gain, or shorter hikes with some climbing; suitable for hikers who exercise regularly. **Strenuous:** hikes of more than four miles or shorter ones that have substantial elevation gain; suitable for hikers who exercise regularly and vigorously.

Open: The times of year when the hiking route is normally usable. Some trails cross "summer" bridges that are removed during the rainy season, and other routes may be subject to periodic closure due to rain or snow. The park visitor centers can provide current status reports, including information about temporary trail closures.

Driving directions: How to reach the trailhead for the hike. We start at some easy-to-locate spot, such as the center of the town of Orick or the Klamath River bridge, and we describe the route from there to the trailhead, indicating all relevant turnoffs and distances. For certain roads that run primarily through one of the parks—such as the Avenue of the Giants, the Newton B. Drury Scenic Parkway, and Howland Hill Road—we provide mileages from each end of the road, listing the distance from the southern end (with the distance from the northern end in parentheses). *If reaching the trailhead requires paying a day-use fee at a park entrance station, or if it requires special caution while driving, we note it here in italics.*

Hike description: We take you from start to finish along the route, noting all junctions and intersections; mentioning key locations, significant plants, and historical or scenic features; and providing mileages whenever appropriate. We sometimes elaborate on plants, places, or historical events of particular interest.

For a longer hike: We describe extensions of the basic route, if relevant. Some of these longer routes require car shuttles, and these are noted.

We conclude the book with 1) summaries about the visitor centers and campgrounds provided by the various parks, and 2) suggestions for further reading.

SAFE, SENSITIVE, AND ENJOYABLE HIKING

Hikers who come to redwood country will find themselves in a temperate climate, moving through low-elevation but sometimes rugged terrain. Thanks to the forest canopy and frequently cloudy weather, they will seldom be exposed to excessive sun. While this environment is less threatening than many others, it is still necessary to exercise proper caution and to prudently prepare for your forays into the redwood forest. The following sections contain recommendations for the equipment, supplies, and precautions you need to take, as well as suggestions for enjoyable and environmentally friendly hiking.

The Ten Essentials: A Systems Approach
1. Navigation (map and compass)
2. Sun protection (sunglasses and sunscreen)
3. Insulation (extra clothing)
4. Illumination (headlamp or flashlight)
5. First-aid supplies
6. Fire (firestarter and matches/lighter)
7. Repair kit and tools (including knife)
8. Nutrition (extra food)
9. Hydration (extra water)
10. Emergency shelter

The authors' recommendations for additional supplies and equipment:
- Waterproof footgear and outerwear—some of the trails cross bridgeless small streams or marshy areas, and it can rain a lot from late fall to early spring.
- Sun protective clothing—a few of the hikes go through open areas—read the trail descriptions closely for clues as to when to take a full-brimmed sun hat (caps do not protect the back of the neck or ears), long pants, and shirts.
- Walking staff or trekking poles—these are remarkably helpful on steep downhill sections of trail, both for maintaining balance and for reducing wear on your knees and other joints.
- Toilet paper and moistened towelettes—use the towelettes anytime you think you may have encountered poison oak.

General precautions:
- Hike with others—a slip on the trail or an encounter with an unfriendly animal can require assistance, and it is best to have

help close at hand. If you do hike alone, be sure to inform a responsible individual of your plans and to check in once you have returned from your hike.

▪ Check trail conditions—inquire at park visitor centers or entrance stations about the hike you plan to take. Are all the trails open? Are any bridges out? Have any potentially dangerous animals been seen in the area? If so, change your plans accordingly.

▪ Lock your car, secure your valuables, and try to park in a public place—make it hard for break-in artists to ruin your hike.

▪ Check the weather—call for a weather report before leaving, take appropriate clothing, and change your plans if necessary.

▪ Listen to your body—it is your best source of information about how well you are meeting the demands of the hike; it will tell you if you should turn around, slacken your pace, or pause to rest. You should heed its commands.

▪ Remember that the trip is the destination—each hike contains a succession of special spots that are worth a short stop. A hurried hike is only half a hike, and it is not the best half by far.

Special hazards

The redwoods parks are, in general, among the safer public places you'll visit. But there are a few potential dangers you should be aware of:

▪ **Wildlife**—Roosevelt elk, black bears, and mountain lions all pose possible threats if you encounter them while hiking. Do not approach any of them and be especially careful not to come between an adult animal and its young. When camping, do not leave food out, and use bear-proof lockers if available. If you encounter a mountain lion, do not run—wave your arms and slowly back away while facing it. If the lion attacks, shout loudly and fight back aggressively. Small children should be held by adults.

▪ **Ticks**—Avoid grassy areas or foliage that may harbor ticks, which can carry Lyme disease. Wear light-colored clothing, tuck in socks and shirts, and inspect your body thoroughly after a hike. You can buy tick removal kits at outdoor stores. If a bull's-eye rash appears at the site of a tick bite, see your physician.

▪ **Poison oak**—Steer clear of three-leafed plants unless you know they are not poison oak. Avoid vines and clumps of foliage. If you think you've been exposed to poison oak, wash the affected area with soap and water or clean it with a moistened towelette. If you develop a rash anyway, try one of the creams or lotions designed to reduce itching.

▪ **Beach hazards**—North Coast beaches sometimes have large "sneaker" waves that can carry you out to sea—be watchful for them. Keep track of tides if you are tidepooling or walking near the shoreline. Earthquakes can cause tsunamis that can reach great heights—keep away from coastlines if a tsunami appears possible.

Protecting the parks (and everything that is in them)

By being thoughtful and following a few basic rules of park etiquette, you can do your part to protect the parks' fragile resources. Here are the authors' recommendations:

▪ **Do not feed wildlife.** Giving food to wildlife not only puts you at risk of attack but also may disrupt natural population patterns. For example, feeding jays and ravens helps increase their populations, which in turn leads to them more frequently attacking marbled murrelet nests and eating the murrelets' eggs and chicks. "A jay fed means a marbled murrelet dead" is a good rhyme to remember.

▪ **Keep pets off park trails.** They are not allowed there to begin with, and for good reason—pets may either become victims of

Coast red elderberry in flower

wildlife attacks or initiate attacks of their own. They can frighten wild creatures with their behavior and sounds, and they can spread disease.

▪ **Pick no plants.** All park plants are protected, some are rare and endangered, and some are poisonous—three good reasons for letting them be.

▪ **Take no artifacts.** Archaeological and historical objects are not to be damaged or removed—it is illegal, disrespectful, and selfish to do so.

▪ **Be courteous and quiet.** Let uphill hikers have the right-of-way. Stand motionless on the downhill side of horses until they pass; speak, in a normal voice, so they will know you are a human. Do not let the sounds of radios, CD players, or your own voice reach a decibel level that will disrupt someone else's hike. In short, be sensitive to the needs of others.

As concerned authors, we have tried to describe trail conditions as accurately as possible and to indicate the approximate difficulty of the various hikes. We have also recommended ways to ensure a safe and pleasant hiking experience. But nothing we write can substitute for the judgment that you exercise while you are out on the trails. Be cautious. Be careful. Be safe.

A NOTE ABOUT SAFETY

Safety is an important concern in all outdoor activities. No guidebook can alert you to every hazard or anticipate the limitations of every reader. Therefore, the descriptions of roads, trails, routes, and natural features in this book are not representations that a particular place or excursion will be safe for your party. When you follow any of the routes described in this book, you assume responsibility for your own safety. Under normal conditions, such excursions require the usual attention to traffic, road and trail conditions, weather, terrain, the capabilities of your party, and other factors. Keeping informed on current conditions and exercising common sense are the keys to a safe, enjoyable outing.

—*The Mountaineers Books*

HUMBOLDT REDWOODS STATE PARK

The largest state redwood park, Humboldt is also the second oldest. It was established in 1922, twenty years after Big Basin State Park was set aside in the Santa Cruz Mountains. Humboldt State Redwood Park, as it was first called, was the result of the combined efforts of local preservationists and the Save-the-Redwoods League. The latter, primarily a group of influential naturalists, academicians, and government officials, began work in 1919 to protect the great groves of redwoods that lay near the confluence of the South Fork and Main Eel Rivers, a forest considered by many to contain the best stands of redwoods found anywhere, but also a forest under attack by the loggers of the Pacific Lumber Company and the operators of "split-stuff layouts," who converted huge old-growth trees into grape stakes, railroad ties, and similar hand-split products. The completion of the

Entrance sign at north end of Avenue of the Giants

Northwestern Pacific Railroad in 1914, followed by that of the Redwood Highway a few years later, opened access to the forest along the South Fork Eel, allowing efficient transport of wood products to the Bay Area while also offering tourists their first chance to easily view the trees. It was a race against time between the tree sawers and tree savers, a race that here, at Humboldt Redwoods, the savers largely won. Within a decade of the park's founding, it had added its centerpiece, the 10,000-acre Rockefeller Forest, and was consolidating a string of smaller groves that lay along the Redwood Highway.

Starting in the 1960s, the League and the park moved to further protect the Rockefeller redwoods by acquiring the entire Bull Creek basin, an area where upstream logging had led to intensified flooding that devastated the Rockefeller Forest. By the 1980s nearly every acre in Bull Creek belonged to the park, and what had once been the three-hundred–person town of Bull Creek was now but a few apple orchards, a couple of houses, and many memories. Today, Humboldt Redwoods State Park encompasses some 52,000 acres of land, about one-third of it old-growth forest of exceptional quality, the rest prairie and cutover timberland.

There are two parts to the park. One is a string of memorial redwood groves that extends along the old Redwood Highway, which is now a scenic alternate route known as the Avenue of the Giants. Starting near Sylvandale in the south, the Avenue runs above the South Fork and Main Eel Rivers for 31 miles, ending just beyond Pepperwood in the north. Along the way are the Hidden Springs Campground, the Burlington Visitor Center and Campground, and the Founders Grove on Dyerville Flat. Between Myers Flat and the Founders Grove, summer bridges connect parkland adjacent to the Avenue with groves on the west side of the South Fork Eel. The visitor center at Burlington contains both a bookstore and an extensive museum; the latter houses a remarkable early-day RV made from a section of redwood log.

Fifteen of the hikes in this book start along the Avenue. Highway 101 runs close to the Avenue, although it is sometimes on the far side of the South Fork Eel. Eight Highway 101 interchanges allow access to the Avenue; at seven of them the two routes are separated by no more than 100 yards. The distance at the eighth, at Weott, is about 0.25 of a mile.

The second section of Humboldt Redwoods is the land contained in the Bull Creek drainage. The Bull Creek canyon is reached by a single route, Mattole Road, which leaves the Avenue and Highway 101 at the Dyerville interchange, near the mouth of the South Fork Eel. At first Mattole Road is a single lane of pavement. It widens to two lanes after passing through the Rockefeller Forest and crossing Bull Creek, some 5.2 miles from its start. Mattole Road then runs up an open section of the canyon, passing the Bull Creek townsite, before climbing to the ridge top and leaving the park at mile 14.4 at Panther Gap. (For a list of park facilities, see Appendix I at the end of the book.)

Nine hikes originate off of Mattole Road, all of them within the first 7.3 miles of the route. Along this stretch are the Big Trees Area, Albee Creek Campground, and Baxter and Hamilton Barn walk-in camps. Mileages to trailheads are given from the start of Mattole Road at its junction with the Avenue.

From the great groves of riverside redwoods along the Avenue to the sweeping hillside prairies above Mattole Road, Humboldt Redwoods State Park offers many scenery-filled hikes. No tour of the North Coast is complete without sampling at least a few of them.

1. F. K. LANE GROVE LOOP

Features ▪	an abandoned stretch of old highway, springtime wildflowers, and good views of big redwoods
Distance ▪	0.45 mile loop
Elevation gain ▪	negligible
Difficulty ▪	easy
Open ▪	all year

Driving directions: Drive to mile 2.9 (28.6) of the Avenue of the Giants, just north of Phillipsville. Turn east into the parking lot for the Franklin K. Lane Grove. The trailhead is at the northern edge of the parking area.

Franklin K. Lane was Secretary of the Interior when he became the first president of the Save-the-Redwoods League in 1919. This grove, which honors him, was originally bisected by the Redwood Highway, but in the late 1930s the road was rerouted west to its present position and the former section of highway kept as a grove access route. Later the old road was abandoned altogether, but vestiges of it still remain, hauntingly visible through the long-encroaching foliage.

A grove dedication plaque for Secretary Lane stands at the north

side of the parking lot. To the right, the hiking route bears northeast through shadowy old-growth redwoods. In about 100 yards the trail divides; go right, ascending onto the roadbed of the old highway. The aging road is littered with downfall and partially covered by plants, but intrepid hikers can explore its course in both directions if they are willing to leave the trail and risk rubbing against poison oak. To the left of the path an aging black and white post—once a highway marker—still stands by the roadside, its luster dimmed by decades of disuse. Long-distance views of large redwoods are visible along the opening made by the old highway.

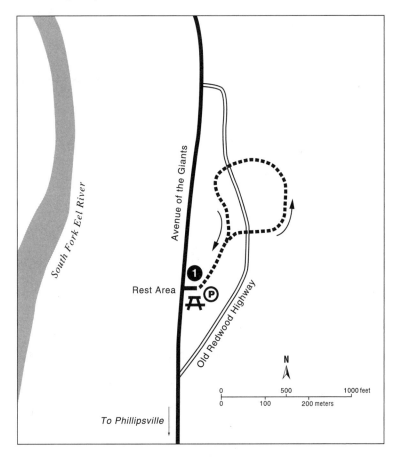

Smooth yellow violet

When the highway came through this area in the 1910s, it first threatened and then helped protect the roadside redwoods. Threatened, because it provided access to the new railroad connection at the town of South Fork, so that "split-stuff" workers—men who hand-cut small sections of redwoods into railroad ties, grape stakes, and the like—could easily transport their products to the rail line for shipment to the Bay Area. Helped protect, because the same highway that was taking out split-up redwoods was also bringing in tourists and conservationists who came to see the trees that were still standing. Appalled at the destruction they beheld, both outsiders—like the founders of the Save-the Redwoods League—and locals rallied to preserve the great highwayside forest by helping to establish what became Humboldt Redwoods State Park.

The trail leaves the roadway and moves east, passing smooth yellow violets before cutting between sections of a 6-foot-diameter log. At mile 0.1 the route turns left at the base of a hillslope, encountering western trillium and Pacific starflower before again turning left. It recrosses the highway at mile 0.3, drops to a lower level of the grove's benchland, and then meets the other end of the loop. A right turn returns you to the trailhead.

9. DRY CREEK LOOP

Features	■ plenty of plants, a bit of climbing, and a dry creek gorge that is sometimes wet
Distance	■ 3.55 miles round trip with small loop (longer hike option available)
Elevation gain	■ 300 feet
Difficulty	■ moderate
Open	■ all year

Driving directions: The trailhead is at mile 7.7 (23.8) of the Avenue of the Giants, north of Miranda. The route starts at a redwood-shaded pullout just off the east side of the Avenue.

Few people hike this trail, which is known officially as the Dry Creek Horse Trail. If you welcome a chance for near solitude and want a bit of exertion soon after arriving on the southern Avenue, this is the place. If it has been a rainy winter, do not be surprised if Dry Creek fails to live up to its name.

Head east on a dirt road, soon entering Dry Creek's narrowing canyon. After passing fat false Solomon's seal and western burning bush, you arrive at an intersection at 0.1 mile. An unnamed foot trail climbs up the hillside to the left, while the horse trail to the right drops from the road toward the creek. Go right, crossing Dry Creek on a substantial wooden bridge. The route climbs the canyonside, where Pacific starflower and vanilla leaf are among the more notable plants. The trail levels and moves along the hillslope through mixed forest, occasionally rising or falling; watch for calypso orchid in spring and the pink-tinted leaves of Pacific dogwood in fall. At 1.1 miles go left at a junction, climbing briskly through patches of two-eyed violet before dropping downhill. The route then meets a fence line and follows it southward, soon turning west and then north. Be alert for more calypso orchids.

You will meet the other branch of the trail at 1.6 miles; turn left, descending on an old roadbed past fetid adder's tongue and more two-eyed violet. After passing a view of the South Fork Eel, the trail abruptly meets the Avenue at mile 2.0. Turn around, regaining the hillside and bearing left in quick

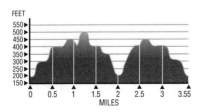

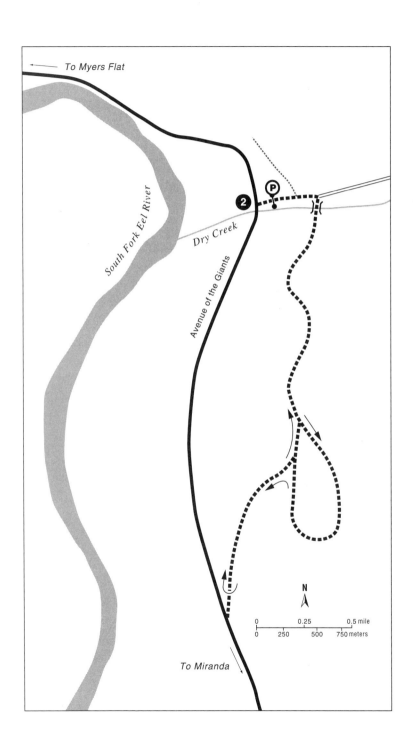

To Myers Flat

South Fork Eel River

Dry Creek

Avenue of the Giants

2

P

To Miranda

N

| 0 | | 0.25 | | 0.5 mile |
| 0 | 250 | 500 | 750 meters |

Dry Creek bridge

succession at two junctions, both near 2.4 miles, that connect to the previously hiked mini loop. Then retrace the first stages of our hike, finishing at mile 3.55.

For a longer hike: Instead of turning back when you reach the Avenue, cross it (watching carefully for traffic) and head south a short distance to the Stephens Grove. Taking the loop trail through this stand of large redwoods adds about a mile to the basic hike.

3. SA-BUG-GAH-NAH LOOP

Features	▪	a beach beneath a rocky point and an amazing assortment of wildflowers
Distance	▪	1.1 miles, including small loop
Elevation gain	▪	100 feet
Difficulty	▪	moderate
Open	▪	all year, except during high water on the South Fork Eel, which can cover part of the trail. (Check with the park visitor center for current conditions during wet weather.)

Driving directions: Drive to mile 11.5 (20) of the Avenue of the Giants. The parking area for the hike, which uses the Hidden Springs Beach Trail, is located on the south side of the road, just east of the entrance to Hidden Springs Beach Campground.

No other hike in the parks offers so much in so short a distance. The focal point is a picturesque, rocky ridgeline that juts sharply southward,

FEET

250 ►
200 ►
150 ►
100 ►

0   0.5   1 1.1
              MILES

forcing the South Fork Eel into a deep bend to pass around it. Now known as Eagle Point, the ridge was more appropriately called *Sa-bug-gah-nah*, or "rock around," by the local Lolahnkok Indians. The cliffs near the end of the point are a botanist's delight, filled with dozens of different plants whose bloom times and color changes provide interest throughout the year.

The parking pullout is next to an aging watering trough made from a scooped-out section of redwood. Its water supply, no longer in frequent use, comes from a pipe that runs through the hollow trunk of the tree just to the left of the trough. Start the hike at the pullout, cautiously walking west some 75 yards along the edge of the Avenue to a wooden railing, where the Hidden Springs Beach Trail commences by dropping on a switchback into mixed forest. The path soon widens, passing California hazel. At 0.15 mile you cross Nelson Road, formerly a section of the original Redwood Highway. On the far side of the road, the trail descends past two-eyed violet and fetid adder's tongue. Tanoak and bigleaf maple rise overhead. These trees are then joined by red alder, black cottonwood, and willows to screen the South Fork, which lies a short distance to the left.

After crossing a stretch of redwood-shaded flat, you reach a junction at the base of the Sa-bug-gah-nah ridgeline at 0.35 mile. The trail to the right leads 50 yards uphill to Nelson Road. Go left, toward the

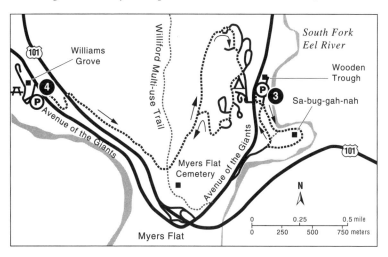

point. Look for Pacific dogwood on the slope uphill to your right. Just ahead, a large rock protrudes from the pathside towards the South Fork. If you stand upon it and look to your left, you'll see a western azalea on the bank a short distance below the trail.

Now the route comes into an open area below the steep cliff near the end of the point. The river sometimes rises enough here to cover the trail, so the next stretch of the path is a walkway made of hand-set, river-resistant stones. In spring and summer it appears that you are now entering an oversized rock garden. On the slope to the right are fat false Solomon's seal, Merten's saxifrage, and poison oak, while Oregon ash, Pacific ninebark, and black cottonwood grow in the riverside rocks to the left. Just ahead is creambush, and, nestled in the rocks above the river, the seldom-seen northern California fuchsia. Across the South Fork, a tall, burned snag towers above the shore. To its left is the site of a Lolahnkok village called Sekontcobandun.

At 0.5 mile the trail leaves the rock walkway and crosses the upper edge of Hidden Springs Beach. The river bend here is a favorite swimming spot in summer, when pond turtles can sometimes be seen sunning themselves on the logs on the far side of the river. To your right is the tip of Sa-bug-gah-nah, shaded by Douglas-fir, canyon live oak, California black oak, California bay, and toyon, which all cling to the cliff. Paintbrush and Pacific Coast iris add summer color to the hillside.

Presently the trail leaves the beach and turns right, climbing back into forest. On the right, nestled among the rocks and poison oak, is another plant rarely seen in the parks, California maidenhair fern. It is closely related to five-finger fern, with which it shares the distinctive delicate black stems that are used in Indian basket making. Also at trailside is the tiny goldenback fern, whose underside is covered with sparkling golden spores. Indian children would press the backs of the fern against their cheeks, creating a sort of glittering temporary tattoo.

Now the trail climbs the western side of Sa-bug-gah-nah. On the flat to the left was once a Lolahnkok village of the same name. A hundred years ago, some fourteen or fifteen house pits were still visible there, but several major floods have either washed away or buried any sign of the site. The path dips briefly toward the flat and then resumes climbing. Watch out for trailside tendrils of poison oak.

At 0.75 mile you crest the grade and then travel for a few yards on the bed of the old county wagon road before reaching Nelson Road.

Opposite: *South Fork Eel and Sa-bug-gah-nah cliff*

Go to the right, following Nelson Road eastward. In 100 feet you pass the access path on your right, which meets the Hidden Springs Beach Trail at the base of the ridgeline. Bigleaf maple and redwood shade the roadway, the former combining with Pacific dogwood and California hazel to provide clusters of fall color. Look on the left for sections of huge redwood logs stacked one upon the other. They form a colossal cribbing that supports the Avenue of the Giants, which is just up the bank. The logs were placed there in the 1930s, when the Redwood Highway was rerouted. As you stand below them, you might consider how much longer they are likely to remain in place. Moving right along, you meet the Hidden Springs Beach Trail at 0.95 mile. Turn left onto it and climb back to the Avenue and thence on to the parking pullout at 1.1 miles.

4. WILLIAMS GROVE–HIDDEN SPRINGS LOOP

Features	▪	a brisk climb, an intricate trip through a campground, and views of both the South Fork Eel and Myers Flat
Distance	▪	5.2 miles, including a loop
Elevation Gain	▪	500 feet
Difficulty	▪	strenuous
Open	▪	all year

Driving directions: Drive to mile 13.5 (18) of the Avenue of the Giants, at the Williams Grove entrance, north of Myers Flat. The trailhead, which is on the east side of the road, has no parking area, although there is a small pullout across the Avenue, just south of the entrance to the Williams Grove day-use area. Parking is available in the grove (admission fee required at entrance station).

Want a nice half-day hike with hill climbing and river viewing? Want to test your orienteering ability in a maze of campground roads? Want to go under the 101 freeway? All of these entertainments are encountered on this eclectic excursion.

The trail departs the eastern edge of the Avenue and heads for the nearby hillside, which it promptly climbs on a series of switchbacks. (See map on page 41.) Various forest wildflowers, redwoods, and lots of evergreen huckleberry cover much of the surroundings. At 0.25

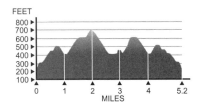

mile the path enters a large culvert that takes it under Highway 101. If you are lucky, a log-laden lumber truck may rumble overhead while you are walking just a few feet beneath it.

East of the freeway the trail resumes its climb, finally leveling in an opening at 0.75 mile. The South Fork Eel and the tiny town of Myers Flat are visible beyond the freeway. Across the river is a section of forest that burned in the fall of 2003. The blaze there mostly attacked the understory, but in a few places it engulfed entire trees, the browned and blackened remnants of which may be seen among the surrounding greenery. You then drop from the opening back into forest, the trail undulating across the hillside. In the vicinity of a small stream at 1.05 miles are western trillium, fat false Solomon's seal, and Pacific starflower. Soon you cross the Williford Multi-Use Trail (M.U.T.) at 1.35 miles. A short distance downhill along this old road is the Myers Flat Cemetery, which is filled with members of the pioneer Myers family. Among the headstones three Myers's names stand out: Ulysses S. Grant Myers, who made a small fortune in the Klondike gold fields, came home, and built the Myers Inn with his money; Nevada C. (California) Jennings, one of Grant's daughters, who was named for not one, but two states; and Leslie R. Myers, whose actual name was Lessor Roosevelt, a tribute offered by his father, Grant, to Teddy the Roughrider. *Note: Due to a dispute with a neighboring landowner, hikers wishing to take a side trip to the cemetery should check with the park visitor center regarding access.*

After crossing the Williford M.U.T. the route climbs beside patches of yerba de selva and Pacific starflower before again reaching level ground. The trail forks at 1.7 miles; bear left, briefly following an old roadbed through mixed second-growth forest and then passing several large Pacific madrones. You then drop downhill and cross a waterline at 2.3 miles. Does the pipe lead from the so-called Hidden Springs? Be watchful during the next section of the hike for other possible sites of the secretive water source.

You soon arrive at a paved road in the Hidden Springs Campground. The way left is for service vehicles, while the way right passes along a turn-around circle and then drops downhill. Those who want to turn back here can retrace their entire route for a 4.8-mile round

South Fork Eel River, near Myers Flat

trip. Those who want to test their navigational skills can proceed on the park road, turning right and descending into the campground, while frequently consulting the hike map.

The campground road soon leads to a junction opposite campsite 74, where you turn right. After passing campsite 77 you should ignore a service road to the right and continue left. In about 75 feet you come to a junction, where you turn right and continue downhill. In about 100 feet you reach a four-way intersection and turn right, going uphill past the campground's amphitheater. (Don't forget

46

to look for signs of the springs.) After passing a lot of stumps you drop to a junction next to campsite 85, where you go right. A short uphill climb brings you to another junction and another right turn, continuing uphill. When you reach the next junction, at 2.9 miles, turn left. In about 200 yards turn right at yet another junction, following the white arrow on the roadway. You crest a hill and drop to the trailhead, which is on the right at campsite 134. Soon the path picks up an old dirt roadbed, which takes you uphill through mixed second-growth forest. At 3.3 miles turn right at a junction with another roadbed, where the way left is conveniently blocked by an old log. You presently reach the trail fork that you met coming in. Turn left here and return along the remainder of the original route, finishing the hike at 5.2 miles.

5. KENT GROVE–SOUTH FORK EEL RIVER LOOP

Features	▪ riverside redwoods and other riparian vegetation above the South Fork Eel
Distance	▪ 1.2 miles, including short loop
Elevation gain	▪ 50 feet
Difficulty	▪ easy
Open	▪ all year

Driving directions: Drive to mile 15.0 (16.5) of the Avenue of the Giants. The trailhead is on the west side of the road.

In this section of the park, the band of land between the bluff-top redwoods and the South Fork Eel River runs like a ribbon of riparian foliage, filled with leafy plants that wave bright green in the winds of summer and turn to golds and yellows in fall. The beach beside the South Fork offers access to the river and views of tall redwoods. This short stroll takes you to a sunny, sandy opening and through a deeply shaded forest.

You begin at the Kent Grove parking area on the west side of the Avenue. In 75 feet the path divides. Turn right, passing lots of bracken fern that crowd into a gap in the forest. In another 100 yards you come to a junction; bear right here at the start of a short loop. Soon western bleeding heart

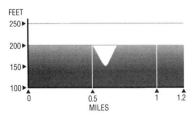

pulses softly by the trailside. A left turn at 0.1 mile passes a side path on the right that leads to the neighboring Mather Grove.

Steven Tyng Mather and William Kent were a pair of patrician preservationists who became activists in the Save-the-Redwoods League. Mather, who was head of the National Park Service, journeyed with another League leader to Eureka in 1919 to promote protecting the trees along the South Fork Eel. There Mather, a former advertising executive, gave a stirring speech to the Eurekeans, pledged a large contribution to support the cause, and, according to one account, then announced that his good but unsuspecting friend, William Kent, would make a similar donation. Kent could well afford the diminishment of

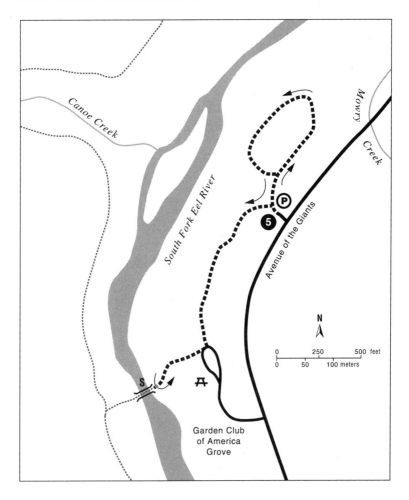

South Fork Eel River, near Garden Club of America Grove

his bank account. A wealthy congressman from Marin County, he had given a redwood-filled canyon there to the federal government, which turned it into Muir Woods National Monument. Later, when the state legislature approved a bill to fund land purchases for Humboldt Redwoods, Kent approached Governor William D. Stephens, who felt that the money would be better spent on schools. "Hell, Bill," shouted Kent, "Close the schools! The kids would love it, and they'd make up the work in a couple of years. It we lose these trees, it will take 2000 years to make them up." Stephens signed the bill.

Bypassing the Mather Grove side trip, the route bears left, encountering large redwoods at least several hundred years old, along with tanoak and bigleaf maple of much later vintage. Now heading south, the trail runs briefly above the South Fork. Look for thin false Solomon's seal, coast red elderberry, and more bracken fern. A spur path to the right leads to an overlook of the river. The main route turns left, moving back into tall timber. At 0.25 mile it meets the beginning of the loop. Turn right, continuing back to the initial trail junction and then bear right to bend around the root end of a massive toppled redwood. Hike through thick forest, ignoring another spur trail to the right. Giant chain fern and then redwood sorrel add their greenery to the flat. Several large stumps stand in the shadows.

Presently the route drops to the parking area for the Garden Club of America Grove. Bear right for 100 feet on the turnaround road and then turn right, taking the wide access path to the South Fork Eel. A profusion of foliage nearly engulfs the trail: rising above coast red elderberry and thimbleberry are willow, Oregon ash, and black cottonwood, the various species linked by wild grape vines that spread like a series of leafy nets over the other plants. In summer this is a spot of shady coolness, while the warmth of dazzling color comes in fall.

The path emerges onto the rocky upper beach of the South Fork Eel, which gives way to sand nearer the shore at 0.55 mile. Here is a place to wander, observe, and perhaps swim, eventually turning around to return, refreshed, to the trailhead.

6. FOREST LODGE

Features	▪ riverside scenery, a once-inhabited goosepen redwood, and the ruins of a historic summer retreat
Distance	▪ 2.0 miles round trip (longer options available)
Elevation gain	▪ 100 feet
Difficulty	▪ moderate
Open	▪ summer only; the seasonal summer bridge across the South Fork Eel is removed during the rainy season (check at the park visitor center for current status)

Driving directions: Drive to mile 16.5 (15) of the Avenue of the Giants. Turn east into the parking lot for the Humboldt Redwoods State Park Visitor Center, or park along the road. The trailhead is on the western side of the Avenue opposite the southern entrance to the parking lot. The hike uses both the Nature Trail and part of the River Trail.

Laura Perrott Mahan was a leader in the early save-the-redwoods movement (see Hike 9). This riverside route takes you to the Perrott family's summer retreat, Forest Lodge, which was eventually taken over by the park.

You begin the hike on the Nature Trail, which lies at the western

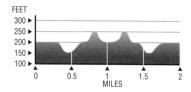

FEET
300 ►
250 ►
200 ►
150 ►
100 ►
0   0.5   1   1.5   2
MILES

end of a crosswalk that connects with the parking lot. The shaded path leads west through a mix of redwoods and large stumps, the latter from the result of small-scale logging done here before the trees could be protected. In 50 yards the Fleischmann Grove Trail forks left, while you bear right, turning north. The loop portion of the Nature Trail begins at 0.1 mile. Go left at the junction, winding through the woods. At another junction, at 0.35 mile, turn left, dropping downhill through a riparian zone of black cottonwood, bigleaf maple, and willow before reaching a pebbly beach. Here you cross the South Fork Eel on a summer bridge, the river's low water level giving no hint that in winter the flow can reach bank to bank. A series of steps leads up the far bank to meet the River Trail at 0.55 mile, onto which you turn right. You soon pass scatterings of vanilla leaf and western trillium.

The trail then drops toward a deep gulch. On the left is a goosepen redwood stump, complete with roof and door frame. The inside of this one-time habitation still contains some pieces of shelving. Cross the gulch at 0.7 mile on a fallen log, to which the park has prudently attached railings. On the far side the trail turns left to climb out of the

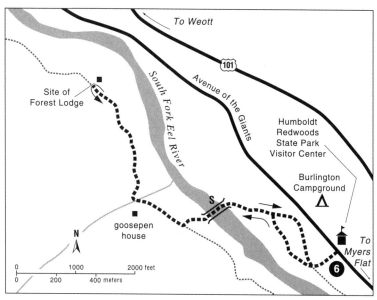

Fireplace and chimney at Forest Lodge

canyon on switchbacks. At the top the route levels and then drops gradually, crossing a small gully before reaching an opening at 1 mile. A fig tree to the right and apple trees to the left indicate that you are at Forest Lodge. To the left, jumbles of vines cover large redwood stumps that formerly had sleeping porches perched on their tops. The orchard once contained two hundred trees—some of the survivors still bear fruit. A side path to the right leads through mock orange, hawthorn, and sweet pea to the foundation and fireplace of Forest Lodge. Beware—poison oak is also present.

The ruins of the lodge repose in the sunlight, telling little of the story of their surroundings. But we have only to hike into the nearby groves of redwoods, which one of the lodge's owners did so much to protect, to understand the spot's true significance.

Even in death Laura Perrott Mahan continued her conservation efforts. She willed her half interest in Forest Lodge to the State of California, which for many years co-owned the property with other members of the Perrott family before gaining full control.

Turn back here, retracing your steps until you rejoin the Nature Trail on the far side of the river. There, at mile 1.6, turn left to complete the loop and follow your approach route out to the Avenue, where the hike ends at 2 miles.

For a longer hike: Instead of turning around at Forest Lodge, you can continue north on the River Trail, reaching Decker Creek in 2.4 miles. Here you can either reverse course or, if you have arranged a car shuttle, pick up the route of Hike 12 and follow its course for an additional 1.45 miles to the parking lot for the Rockefeller Loop.

7. BURLINGTON-GOULD

Features ■	a hillside ramble, summer lilies, and a historic road and homesite
Distance ■	2.5 miles round trip
Elevation gain ■	100 feet
Difficulty ■	moderate
Open ■	all year

Driving directions: Drive to Burlington, mile 16.5 (15.0) of the Avenue of the Giants, and turn east into the parking lot for the Humboldt Redwoods State Park Visitor Center. The hike begins at the northeast corner of the parking lot. Most of it is on the Burlington-Weott Trail.

This hillside hike follows parts of the old county road north from Burlington before reaching the site of the summer home of the Gould family, which once owned much of upper Bull Creek watershed.

After leaving the parking lot, walk some 75 feet towards the visitor center on a paved pathway, turning left in front the building and crossing a streamlet as you enter a stand of redwoods. The walkway then ends at one of the Burlington Campground's paved roads. Turn right here and follow the road past large stumps and beneath a covering of second-growth trees. Bear right on the roads until you reach campsite 26 at 0.35 mile. Turn right onto the trail that begins just past the campsite. You soon cross the gorge of Robinson Creek on a stout wooden bridge. Just past the bridge, bear right at a junction; the way left leads to the River Trail and Hike 6. Look for vanilla leaf and red huckleberry near the pathside.

At mile 0.5 the route crosses a paved park maintenance road and then begins to climb uphill on the bed of the old wagon road. Here in springtime you will find the pale blooms of Pacific dogwood, western trillium, fat false Solomon's seal, redwood inside-out flower, and, most noticeably, windflower. The wide path rises up the hillside, but the grade soon diminishes. Highway 101 is audible, and then visible, upslope.

At 0.75 mile the trail reaches an opening where the trail has

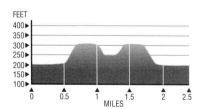

FEET
400►
350►
300►
250►
200►
150►
100►

0   0.5   1   1.5   2   2.5
MILES

been rebuilt following a landslide. Reenter forest and take a switchback downhill. Soon you cross a small wooden bridge, pass through lots of evergreen huckleberry, and then, at 0.9 mile, you come to a cathedral group of four redwoods on the left. Here, in season, are several redwood lilies and lots of fat false Solomon's seal. Just ahead, a picturesque bridge spans a small stream next to the base of a medium-size redwood. The trail drops downhill, passing a large tanoak to the left, and then levels. The Avenue is some 200 feet below.

You arrive at an intersection at 1.2 miles. The way left descends to the Avenue, across which lies Gould Bar, a popular swimming spot. The main trail continues straight ahead, soon arriving at the town of

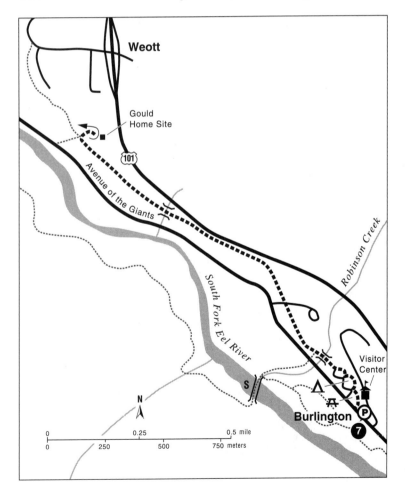

Pacific dogwood

Weott. Your route turns right, climbing along what was once the drive-way to the Gould house. You soon reach the homesite, marked now only by a cleared, level area, and, to the right, a section of stone wall and concrete foundation. Half a century ago Eureka realtor Chauncey Gould, his wife Mabel, and their family would summer here, while also spending time at their Bull Creek Ranch, situated high up in the drainage on the far side of Grasshopper Peak, several miles above the town of Bull Creek.

In 1960 the Gould's trailside property was the subject of a lawsuit. The state public works department sued to condemn the land, part of which was needed as a right-of-way for the new 101 freeway. The state offered the Goulds $4200, but Chauncey and Mabel demanded $25,000, claiming that the recently logged property could be used for homesite development. The jury came all the way down from Eureka to view the area in question, and they agreed with the Goulds that the state had misvalued the property. In fact, the jury concluded, the dam-aged land was worth only $3500, which is what it awarded Chauncey and Mabel.

Wiser in the realities of real estate, you leave the Gould homesite and retrace your route to the trailhead.

8. BIG CUT

Features	▪	forest wildflowers, a bluff-side view of the South Fork Eel, and an attractive piece of park architecture
Distance	▪	2.4 miles round trip, including a mini loop (longer hike option available)
Elevation gain	▪	250 feet
Difficulty	▪	moderate
Open	▪	all year

Driving directions: Drive to mile 20.2 (11.3) of the Avenue of the Giants. The trailhead is at a pullout for the Mahan Plaque Loop on the east side of the road.

This route takes you high above the South Fork Eel and then almost next to it. In between, you travel under the 101 freeway and across the Avenue of the Giants. Plenty of redwood forest plants and a charming picnic area make this a great hike for sampling the charms of Humboldt Redwoods.

The route begins on the Mahan Plaque Loop (see Hike 9), crossing the southern end of Dyerville Flat. In quick succession you bear right at two junctions with the northern end of the loop and then reach another junction at the base of a hillslope. Here you turn right, departing the Mahan Plaque Loop, and begin ascending the hillside. In spring the pathway is bordered by a profusion of attractive plants—western coltsfoot, California spikenard, wild ginger, and vanilla leaf are among the most notable. The trail zigzags up the steep slope, offering views of the redwood-filled flat below.

At 0.2 mile the trail levels, crosses a section of drainage pipe, and comes out onto one of the broad terraces of Big Cut. Here the end of Duckett Bluff was lopped off to make room for the 101 freeway, and the face of the cut was terraced. Look for two red-berried plants—toyon and Pacific madrone. A view of the South Fork Eel opens to the right. The trail crosses a second drainage pipe at 0.4 mile and then narrows as it reenters forest. Soon the route drops, reaching another level of

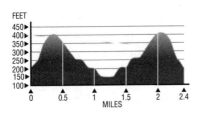

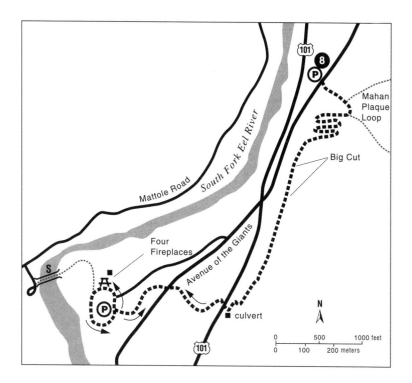

the terrace before again descending to reach Highway 101 at 0.75 mile. Here a large culvert, meant for people, not water, takes you under the highway and into old-growth redwoods.

At 0.85 mile the route crosses the Avenue of the Giants. *Use extreme caution when making the crossing.* California hazel and tanoak grow beneath the big trees as the trail winds its way westward. At mile 1.05 turn right at a junction; notice the striking full-length views of nearby redwoods. In 50 yards you reach the paved access road for the Women's Federation Grove. Turn left and follow the road a hundred yards to the grove picnic area on your right. The first attraction here is the Hearthstone, otherwise known as the Four Fireplaces, a wood and stone construction designed by architect Julia Morgan, best known for her work at San Simeon's Hearst Castle. Here her design is on a smaller scale, but it is nonetheless striking: four stone fireplaces joined around a single chimney, each hearth covered by a wooden gabled roof, the space above each mantle containing a circular stone that bears an edifying inscription. To arrive here on a fall day, the forest golden with bigleaf maples and a wisp of gray smoke rising from the chimney, is to experience the park at its seasonal best.

Nearby are a pair of enormous picnic tables, each with proportionately large benches, all milled from old-growth redwood in the 1930s. They have since served for thousands of redwood-shaded repasts. A trail near the picnic tables drops down to a summer bridge crossing of the South Fork Eel.

Your way is now along the access road, passing through a parking lot that offers views of the river, and on to a turnaround circle at 1.25 miles. Bear left at the circle and turn left onto the trail that exits the turnaround in about 75 feet. Follow this route back through the Federation forest until you arrive at a junction. Here you are reunited with the trail over Big Cut. Turn right and return to the trailhead at 2.4 miles.

For a longer hike: In summer, take the river access trail at the Federation Grove picnic area, dropping in 100 yards to the South Fork Eel, which you cross on a summer bridge. On the far bank, take the trail up the bluff to the Rockefeller Loop parking area and from there commence either Hike 11 or Hike 12, eventually retracing your way back to the Federation Grove and the trailhead.

The Four Fireplaces

9. MAHAN PLAQUE LOOP

Features ■	the famed redwoods of Dyerville Flat and a monument to a pair of early-day tree savers
Distance ■	0.6 mile loop
Elevation gain ■	negligible
Difficulty ■	easy
Open ■	all year

Driving directions: Drive to mile 20.2 (11.3) of the Avenue of the Giants. The trailhead is at a pullout on the east side of the road.

In the 1920s, Dyerville Flat was a prize hotly contested by conservationists and the Pacific Lumber Company. The conservationists triumphed, thanks in large part to the crusading couple who are honored at a pathside monument here.

The trail starts at a row of stobbers next to the parking pullout, immediately running eastward across the redwood-filled flat. Redwood sorrel covers much of the ground, with sword fern, giant chain fern, and bracken fern providing additional greenery. In 100 feet bear right at a junction, and then promptly bear right again at a second junction. The route runs past some small tanoak and reaches the base of a hillside, where the Big Cut Trail (see Hike 8) forks right. Go left, winding among numerous trees and logs while remaining close to the hillside. After avoiding a social trail that goes to the left at 0.2 mile, you come to the Mahan Plaque, set in a large rock that rests between two even larger stumps.

The plaque honors Laura Perrott Mahan and her attorney husband, James, who were activists in the Humboldt County save-the-redwoods movement during the 1920s. The Pacific Lumber Company, which owned the flat at that time, began to secretly cut a railroad right-of-way here in the fall of 1924. The plan was to run a spur line from the train station at the nearby town of South Fork, cut across the southern end of the flat, bridge the South Fork Eel, and continue the line into the rich redwood forest of lower Bull Creek. Rumors of the cutting reached the

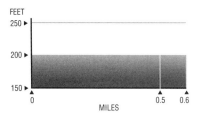

Mahans, who drove down from Eureka to take a look. Finding the log-gers busy at work, the couple flashed the news to the local papers. Public reaction was swift and decisive: within a few months the county board of supervisors unanimously approved a Save-the-Redwoods League plan to acquire the land. Although negotiations dragged on for over six years, the Dyerville and Bull Creek Flats finally became part of the park in 1931. The line of stumps you pass while on the trail is—thanks in large part to the Mahans—as far as the tree choppers from Pacific Lumber ever got.

The trail turns sharply to the left just past the monument, wend-ing its way among giant trees that will never see the inside of a mill. At 0.4 mile a walk-through goosepen on the right will delight children at

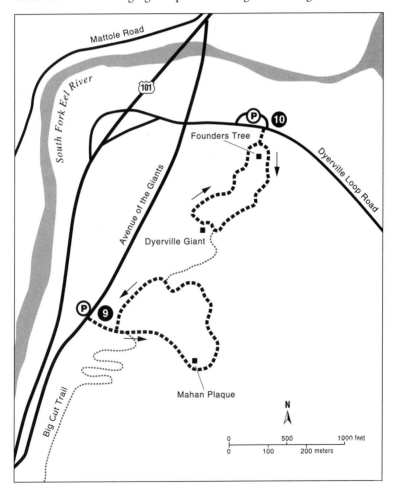

Goosepen redwood, Mahan Plaque Loop

least as much as any geese. A side trail to the right at 0.5 mile connects with the Founders Grove Loop (see Hike 10). Bear left here, passing through the halves of a large log and meeting the start of the trail. Turn right at the junction and arrive back at the trailhead.

10. FOUNDERS GROVE LOOP

Features	■ the skyscraping Founders Tree and what is probably the world's largest redwood log—the Dyerville Giant
Distance	■ 0.5 mile loop
Elevation gain	■ negligible
Difficulty	■ easy
Open	■ all year

Driving directions: Drive to mile 20.6 (10.9) of the Avenue of the Giants. At an intersection with Dyerville Loop Road, turn east. In 100 yards turn left into the Founders Grove parking lot. Take the crosswalk near the restrooms, crossing Dyerville Loop Road. The hike starts at the southern side of the road.

In 1917 three participants in the annual Bohemian Club gathering on the Russian River, having heard reports of "a forest wall reported to have mystery and charm unique among the living works of creation," left their summer retreat and drove north until they reached their "wall," which consisted of the gigantic redwoods of the Bull Creek and Dyerville Flats. The three men were all well-known naturalists: Madison Grant, the founder of the New York Zoological Society; Henry Fairfield Osborne, president of the American Museum of Natural History; and John C. Merriam, a professor of paleontology who later became president of the Carnegie Institution. The forest they found on the flats exceeded their already high expectations, and its discovery prompted them to spend the next several months trying in vain to gain government protection of the great riverside groves. Finally the men decided that the work would have to be initiated privately, and so they joined with a group of prestigious kindred spirits to start the Save-the-Redwoods League. The three founders of the League are commemorated by a 350-foot-plus redwood on the flats where they "found" their forest.

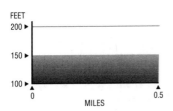

A row of stobbers lines the way south from the crosswalk. (See map on page 60.) In 75 feet you bear left at a junction with the access trail that leads from the bus parking area. In another 100 feet you bend right and are faced with the tall spire of the Founders Tree, whose trunk soars skyward unimpeded by limbs for a great distance, finally giving way to a cloud of dark green foliage. A boardwalk encircles the tree, allowing observers to take a closer look without damaging the tree's roots.

Directly in front of the tree the path divides. Go left, bearing left again in 50 feet where a railed trail heads right to provide a view of the back of the Founders Tree. Your way is along the "Founders Freeway," a wide, level path that is probably trod by more feet than any other route in the redwood parks. It winds past many large redwoods, including a walk-through goosepen to the left at 0.1 mile. Sword ferns abound among the trees, joined by redwood sorrel, Hooker's fairybell, lady fern, and bracken fern. At 0.2 mile a collection of large fallen redwoods has left an opening in the forest cover, allowing some coast red elderberry a bit of space.

Soon the trail reaches a junction. The way left leads to the Mahan Plaque Loop (see Hike 9). Stay to the right. Immediately ahead is the enormous root end of the Dyerville Giant. A huge hole where the tree

The downed Dyerville Giant

stood is now railed off, and the trail conveniently runs along the right side of the Giant's trunk for 200 feet before turning to complete its loop.

The Dyerville Giant was an especially thick-trunked redwood that many people suspected of being the world's tallest tree, but up until March 1991 it had been impossible to obtain an exact measurement. After that, the Giant's height was no longer an issue, for it toppled to earth not long after being hit by a falling neighboring redwood. The Giant's crash to earth was so loud that nearby residents thought it was a train wreck, which wasn't a bad guess—the mammoth redwood probably weighed about as much as any locomotive. When the Giant fell, its top smashed into another tree and shattered, effectively eliminating any chance for a post-mortem measurement. Estimates were nonetheless made and were in the 370-foot range, which would indeed have given the Giant the tallest tree award if it had remained standing.

Departing what is now the Dyerville Log, the trail heads north, returning to the Founders Tree to complete the loop. Retrace your approach route to the parking lot.

11. ROCKEFELLER LOOP

Features ■	a series of statuesque redwoods and a monument to the big trees' biggest benefactor
Distance ■	0.65 mile loop (longer option available)
Elevation gain ■	negligible
Difficulty ■	easy
Open ■	all year

Driving directions: Drive west to mile 1.4 of Mattole Road. Turn left onto the steep and narrow access road for the Rockefeller Loop and travel 0.1 mile to the trailhead parking lot.

When the Save-the-Redwoods League took John D. Rockefeller Jr. on a tour of the lower Bull Creek Flat, they did so in an open car. After staring skyward at hundreds of redwoods, Rockefeller was impressed enough to write the League a check for a million dollars. But even this left the League still short of funds, so the heir to the Standard Oil fortune later followed up with another million, providing much of the money necessary to purchase the finest stand of redwoods found anywhere—over 10,000 acres of towering trees that grew in the rich soils

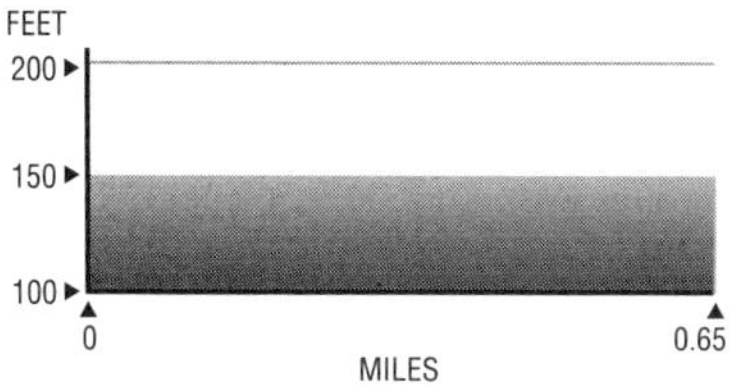

near the mouth of Bull Creek. The League later obligingly dedicated the forest to Rockefeller, so that a wealth of redwoods now bears the name of one of America's wealthiest families.

The route begins at the southwestern edge of the parking lot; ignore the nearby trail sign, which refers to backcountry destinations far from the range of your hike. In 100 feet bear right when the path divides to form its loop. You now move through a thick growth of redwood sorrel, above which tower Rockefelleresque redwoods. Presently you pass through a cut in a low-lying log and immediately turn left, avoiding the social trail to the right. A short climb then takes you to a higher level of the benchland. Notice the 6-inch-diameter tree limb that juts upward some 8 feet above where it is implanted in the ground. Loggers call such potentially lethal limbs "widow makers."

At 0.25 mile is a junction. The route to the right connects with

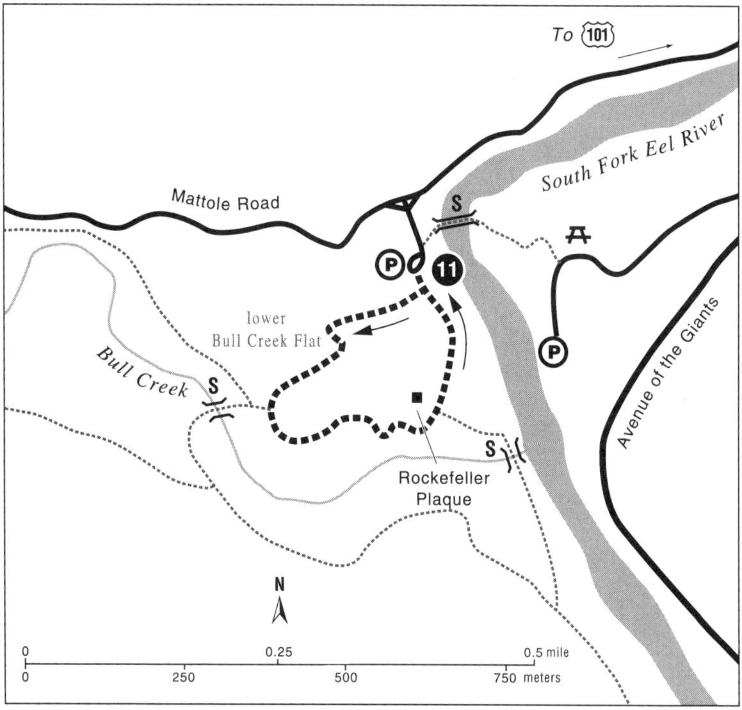

Redwood stump sprouts

the Bull Creek and River Trails, the latter of which you travel on Hike 12. Bear left. Now the redwoods become especially striking; several of them have large, drooping burls, while others are surrounded by collections of small redwood sprouts waiting to become the next millennium's giants. You catch a glimpse of Bull Creek downhill to the right at 0.35 mile, and then arrive at the Rockefeller dedication plaque to the left. Just ahead a spur trail to the right leads a few hundred feet to the mouth of Bull Creek. Use caution if you follow its steep course down to the creek. Go left under an enormous redwood log that has had a section of its lower side removed to accommodate passage. Zigzag around a pair of large fallen redwoods, pass an abandoned spur trail (this one to the South Fork Eel to the right), and complete the loop. A right turn here takes you to the parking lot at 0.65 mile.

For a longer hike: At the 0.25-mile junction, turn right instead of left and go to Decker Creek on Hike 12. This adds 2.1 miles to the trip.

12. DECKER CREEK

Features	▪	two picturesque streams and a hillside ramble among the redwoods
Distance	▪	2.75 miles round trip with short loop (longer options available)
Elevation gain	▪	100 feet
Difficulty	▪	moderate
Open	▪	summer only (the bridge across Bull Creek is removed during the rainy season—check with the park visitor center for status)

Driving directions: Drive west to mile 1.4 of Mattole Road. Turn left onto the access road for the Rockefeller Loop and travel 0.1 mile to the trailhead parking lot.

This hike takes you along the northernmost section of the park's River Trail, which runs along the west bank of the South Fork Eel. The fern-filled canyon of secluded Decker Creek provides an especially appealing destination.

You begin the hike at the southern edge of the parking lot by starting on the first part of the Rockefeller Loop. Bear right at the first junction and wind through the forest until you reach a second junction at 0.25 mile, where you turn right. You promptly pass two paths on your right that soon join to form part of the Bull Creek Flats Trail. Bearing left, you drop to Bull Creek, passing giant chain fern at the base of the bank on your left. Cross the creek on a summer bridge. Notice the view upstream to your right, where Bull Creek descends along its rocky bed while framed by the towering trees of the Rockefeller Forest.

After rising out of the creek canyon, the trail crosses a short section of benchland and then climbs the hillside, reaching a junction at 0.45 mile. To the right is the southern section of the Bull Creek Flats Trail. Go left, following the River Trail as it cuts across the hillside. Mixed in with the redwoods are Douglas-fir and tanoak. You drop to a flat at 0.85 mile, passing a spur trail to your left. Your route then winds across another benchland, passing a leafy canopy of California hazel and Pacific dogwood at 1.1 miles. Soon the trail begins a gradual descent that brings you, at 1.3 miles, to deeply shaded Decker Creek. A log bridge (with railing) spans the picturesque stream. To the right is a tangle of fallen redwoods and several lovely, leafy vine maples. To the left are good views of a profusion of lady and five-fingered ferns that embellish the canyonside.

Five-fingered fern (*Adiantum aleuticum*), also known as maidenhair fern, is a delicate, softly green plant that is striking from a distance and even more appealing when seen closer up. A set of several (sometimes, but not always, five) fronds spreads outward on thin black stems, the fronds splaying widely like fingers on a very large hand. The fronds are composed of rows of frilly pinnae (the individual small green

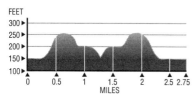

FEET
300 ▶
250 ▶
200 ▶
150 ▶
100 ▶

0   0.5   1   1.5   2   2.5 2.75
MILES

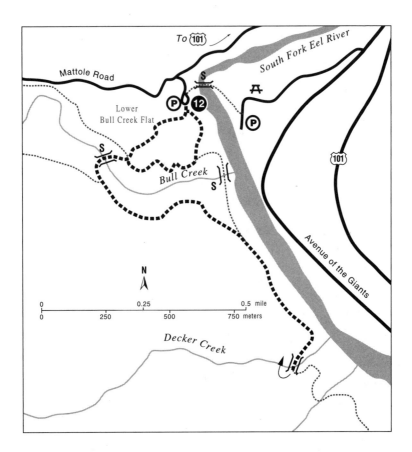

sections that grow off each stem) that appear to have a texture like velvet. The dark stems were used by local Indians for forming patterns in their basketry work. Five-finger ferns love water, and they will often be seen adorning the banks of stream canyons. They are most famously exhibited in Prairie Creek Redwoods State Park at Fern Canyon (see Hike 40), but here they delightfully decorate little-known Decker Creek in much less crowded surroundings.

The canyon makes a good turnaround point for the hike, so retrace your route to the junction with the Rockefeller Loop at 2.35 miles. A right turn here completes the loop at the parking area.

For a longer hike: Your route along the South Fork can be extended by continuing south along the River Trail, reaching the ruins of Forest

Opposite: Bull Creek, looking upstream

Lodge in an additional 2.4 miles. From there you can either backtrack to Decker Creek and complete the hike described above, or, if a car shuttle is available, take the return route of Hike 7 to the visitor center at Burlington, which is 3.4 miles from Decker Creek.

13. LOOK PRAIRIE

Features ▪	a picturesque hillside grassland, an old homestead site, and a monumental bigleaf maple
Distance ▪	3.2 miles round trip (longer option available)
Elevation gain ▪	850 feet
Difficulty ▪	strenuous
Open ▪	all year

Driving directions: Drive to mile 4.0 of Mattole Road. The hike departs from a parking area on the northern side of road.

A long, cascading hillside prairie provides much of the scenery on this route. It was named for the Look family—Allan, Sara, and their six sons—who ranched there from the late nineteenth century to 1905. Most maps show the lower section of grassland as Luke Prairie, close enough to Look that it might seem a misprint, but it is actually the name of a later resident, Bill Luke. When the Lukes lived there in the 1940s, the original ranch house burned and had to be rebuilt. The Look Prairie Barn, built by Allan and his sons, lasted much longer, but it, too, burned in the 1990s. By then the second ranch house was also gone, and today only a few fruit trees, a scattering of flowers, and some charred timbers from the barn remain.

From the parking area follow Look Prairie Road past a locked park gate, moving gradually uphill beneath redwoods. California hazels cover the slope to the right. The road skirts the edge of Luke Prairie, switchbacking and climbing more steeply as both California black oak and Oregon white oak spread their leafy limbs overhead. At 0.4 mile the road briefly enters the prairie and then plunges back into woods. The air

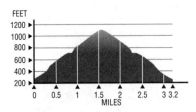

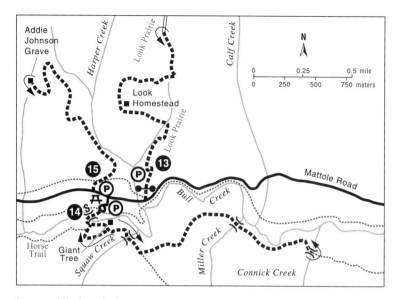

here is filled with the scent of California bay. Soon the road crosses a sidehill prairie, passes a lone fruit tree, and then briefly reenters forest, making a last turn before leveling and arriving at the location of the Look homestead at 0.8 mile. To the left are a garden remnant and the location of the Look and Luke houses. Just ahead, in the grassland across the road from a fallen oak, was the lovely Look Prairie Barn, a small, gracefully proportioned structure made of hand-hewn redwood timbers and shakes.

After leaving the barn site, the road dips briefly, passes a watering trough, and then turns to cross the middle of the prairie. A few fruit trees and a solitary chestnut still rise from the grass to the right, while ahead, a large bigleaf maple stands in solitary splendor by the roadside. In summer, popcorn flower pops up from the next section of the roadbed. At 1.2 miles the route leaves the eastern side of the prairie, moving into a mixed evergreen forest with a stream canyon to the right. Here, near the roadside in spring, grow two-eyed violet and calypso orchid. The road levels briefly and Look Prairie then reappears, coming down to meet the road, left, at 1.6 miles. You may climb out into the upper end of the grassland if you choose (always being mindful of ticks) and look out across Look Prairie and the Bull Creek canyon at the rising bulk of forested Grasshopper Peak. If you'd like a bit more adventure, hike cautiously down the prairie, soon dropping steeply, and regain the road

Bigleaf maple, Look Prairie

near the orchard. Otherwise, return the way you came, reaching the trailhead at 3.2 miles.

For a longer hike: Continue on up Look Prairie Road, climbing through mixed forest, until you reach Peavine Road at 3.4 miles. From there, return down Look Prairie Road, adding 3.6 miles to your hike.

14. BULL CREEK FLATS

Features ■	the Giant Tree, many other world-class redwoods, and views of Bull Creek
Distance ■	3.55 miles round trip (longer option available)
Elevation gain ■	negligible
Difficulty ■	moderate
Open ■	summer only (the bridge across Bull Creek is removed for the rainy season—check at the park visitor center for current status)

Driving directions: Drive to mile 4.4 of Mattole Road. Turn south onto the access road for the Big Trees Area and drive 0.1 mile to a parking lot, where the hiking route departs to the southwest.

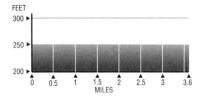

The Bull Creek Flats Trail is an 8-mile loop that traverses most of the Rockefeller Forest. This hike takes you through the most memorable section of the trail, filled with towering trees and large logs, avoiding the noisier northern part of the loop, which runs near Mattole Road.

Begin the hike just west of a signboard at the edge of the Big Tree Area parking lot, angling downhill to the summer bridge across Bull Creek. (See map on page 71.) Red alder and willow fringe the rocky creekbed, which is only moderately moistened in summer but capable of running high, wide, and ugly in winter, having recently washed away a "permanent" bridge that was thought to be safe from any flood. In years past, when logging and fires had removed many of the trees in the upper basin, the creek was even more rambunctious, perhaps never more so than in December 1955, when a tremendous storm hit the North Coast and dropped more than 21 inches of rain in a single day just over the ridge, at the hamlet of Honeydew, and soaking the soil past its absorption capacity. The excess water soon poured off the denuded hillslopes, mixing into a slurry of mud, rocks, and logging debris that surged down the canyon and swept away almost all that stood before it. Don Gould, whose ranch lay far up Bull Creek, found himself racing down Mattole Road, trying to make it out of the canyon ahead of the torrent. With water already flooding the roadway, Gould crossed Bull Creek on the bridge just west of the Rockefeller Forest. Moments later, a huge logjam at the nearby Bee River Mill broke up, sending a wall of water and two million board feet of timber down the creek, smashing the bridge into fragments and hitting the Rockefeller redwoods. The bridge could be replaced in a matter of months, but the more than five hundred trees that were lost would not be replaced for centuries. Surveying the damage, the state developed a plan to protect the remaining trees by acquiring all the land in the drainage, thus halting the timber cutting that so magnified the effects of the flood. Gould's ranch was among the many places purchased by the park, but after the ride of his life one dark December night, he probably was ready to bid good-bye to Bull Creek.

On the far side of the summer bridge bear left past two trail junctions to reach, mile 0.1, the Giant Tree, a massive specimen that was determined to be the National Champion Redwood in 1991. Faced with this obstacle, the path veers to the right, winding through a mixed forest. At mile 0.2 we turn left at a junction with the Horse Trail.

A sturdy wooden bridge spans Squaw Creek. The stream's unfortunate name (historically "squaw" was a derogatory term for Indian women) derives from an even more unfortunate event—a group of Indians were massacred here by whites, probably in the 1850s or 1860s.

Just ahead is a junction. The way right climbs to historic Johnson Tie Camp, where split redwood products, including railroad ties, were prepared up until the 1950s. You go left, however, passing sugar scoop and salal before reaching an opening at 0.7 mile where several large redwoods have crashed to earth. At 0.8 mile the trail passes along a long corridor formed by two more fallen redwoods. A log bridge spans the gorge of minute Miller Creek at 1.2 miles and the trail leaves the forest at 1.4 miles to cross a small meadow. Western blue flax speckles the grass in spring, while blueblossom and snowbrush scent the surroundings. The route then briefly runs close to Bull Creek, pushed there by a steep slope to the right. After reentering forest, you reach another gorge-spanning bridge, this one over Connick Creek. Here we reverse course, bearing right at the Johnson Tie Camp Trail junction, recrossing Square Creek, and continuing to the Horse Trail junction at mile 3.1, where

Getting a grip on the Giant Tree

we now go left, following the Horse Trail as it passes among large redwoods. At mile 3.3 we leave the Horse Trail, turning right at a junction. Our route winds through fallen redwoods, mile 3.5, to reach another junction where we bear left. Just to the left is the former Flatiron Tree, a once-tilted redwood whose oddly shaped base resulted from a buttress that it grew (unsuccessfully, as it turned out) to keep from toppling groundward. We then meet our original trail, where we turn left to recross Bull Creek and reach the trailhead at 3.55 miles.

For a longer hike: Continue east on the Bull Creek Flats Trail, turning left at a junction with the River Trail, crossing Bull Creek on a summer bridge, and then bearing left at a junction near the top of the bluff. You follow the creek upstream, bearing left at one junction, to return to the Big Trees Area parking lot after adding about 6.25 miles to the hike.

15. ADDIE JOHNSON GRAVE

Features	▪	a shaded stream canyon and a pioneer woman's grave
Distance	▪	2.3 miles round trip
Elevation gain	▪	600 feet
Difficulty	▪	moderate
Open	▪	all year

Driving directions: Drive to mile 4.4 of Mattole Road, just west of the turnoff to the Big Tree Area. The trail starts at an unmarked parking area on the north side of the road.

A lost lamb originally led the way to the peaceful ridge-top spot where this hike concludes. Now you can take a shaded park trail to the gravesite of the lamb's long-departed owner.

You start in the fabled Rockefeller Forest, the largest grove of old-growth redwoods in the world. (See map on page 71.) While staring skyward at their soaring trunks you're likely to miss another red-wooded tree—a small, moss-covered Pacific yew (*Taxus brevifolia*) that stands forlornly just to the right of the path a few yards from its start. It is hard to believe that such an unassuming specimen is part of a proud heritage; however, yews have

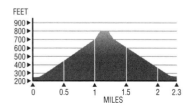

Addie Johnson's grave

long made important contributions to humankind. In 1346 longbows made of yew wood allowed the English archers of Edward III to devastatingly defeat the French army at the battle of Crécy, giving Edward a signal victory and establishing the longbow as the age's most formidable weapon. Much more recently, a potent anti-cancer substance called taxol has been derived from yew bark, proving the continuing worth of the members of the *Taxus* family.

After 50 yards the path meets the Horse Trail, an equestrian/hiker route that runs along the northern edge of the flat. The hiking route turns right, following the Horse Trail until mile 0.1, where you branch left at a fork. At 0.2 mile you head into the canyon of Harper Creek. As you gradually climb the slope the creek sends its splashing sound upward, raucously noisy in winter and spring, more subdued during the dry months.

The trail rises along the hillside through mixed forest until it reaches a flat at 0.7 mile. The small-leaved shrub that fills much of the area is evergreen huckleberry, one of the most common plants in the redwood forest. Look also for the dusty green leaves and grayish bark of tanoak, another common understory resident.

At 0.9 mile you pass a second Pacific yew, this one overhanging the trail from its perch on the bank to the left. A switchback then takes the route south. Just ahead the path is bordered by one of the park's earliest blooming flowers. If you are lucky enough to be here in February, you'll see the delicately pointed, cream- and wine-colored petals of the fetid adder's tongue (*Scoliopus bigelovii*), whose forbidding name refers not only to its shape but also to its distinctive smell, which some beholders have likened to rotting meat. The odor is actually part of the plant's survival strategy. Since fetid adder's tongue blooms too early for the normal pollinators to be present, it needs to attract flies to do the job, and, as we all know, the scents preferred by flies are quite different from those preferred by most other species, including humans.

By way of compensation, the next plant you meet along the trail has a far more pleasant aroma—the California bay is sometimes known as both pepperwood and laurel, and its sharply pointed, dark green leaves suffuse the air with a strong but strangely appealing scent.

You then make a switchback to the right and come out on a ridgeline. To the left are intermittent views of a steeply sloping prairie and, at 1.1 miles, of Grasshopper Peak. Both Oregon white oak and California black oak border the path, while French broom, an invasive alien, encroaches the ridge top from the downslope prairie.

The trail then reaches a shaded knoll, where a low picket fence surrounds a grave marker and a pair of tall cypress trees. Buried here is Addie Johnson, who homesteaded on the nearby prairie with her husband Tosaldo in 1872. One day, while searching for a lost lamb, Addie hiked to this promontory, which looked down on the family homestead. She fell in love with the spot and told her husband that she would like to be buried here when she passed away. Only a few months later a grieving Tosaldo had to honor her request after Addie died in childbirth. The trail ends, like Addie's story, at her gravesite.

The way back follows the same route, returning you to the parking area at 2.3 miles.

16. ALBEE-THORNTON

Features ▪	a redwood-shaded creek, steep hillside prairies, and a boulder-strewn stand of mixed old-growth forest
Distance ▪	7.9 miles round trip (longer option available)
Elevation gain ▪	1300 feet
Difficulty ▪	strenuous
Open ▪	all year (snow may cover the upper section of the hike in winter—check at the park visitor center for current conditions)

Driving directions: Drive to mile 5.0 of Mattole Road. Park along the roadside opposite the access road to Albee Creek Campground. The hike starts at the access road. Most of the route is on the Thornton Equestrian/Hiker Trail.

Until recently Thornton Road was one of the steepest, most heavily rutted routes in the park, enjoyed by gonzo mountain bikers more than hikers. Now most of the road has been removed and replaced by a switchbacking trail of gentle gradient, along which lies the destination for this hike, a magical enclave of uncut hillside forest.

Begin on the north side of Mattole Road by following the paved access road to the Albee Creek Campground. The giant trees of the Rockefeller Forest shade some of the most spectacular springtime flowers of the redwoods. Watch the roadside for western trillium, redwood violet, fetid adder's tongue, and, most especially, calypso orchid. At 0.25 mile the road crosses the Horse Trail, which is open to both equestrians and hikers. You should find many adder's tongues and orchids just to the right along this route.

The campground road then bends left, passes a side road to the right and crosses Albee Creek on a wooden bridge. Turn right just past the bridge onto a campground road that runs beside Albee Creek. Local mail carrier John Albee provided the creek with his name, and his apple orchard lies at the southern side of the campground. Albee's property was later taken over by the Thornton family, who provided the extremely steep logging road that ran up to the ridge with *their* name. Hugh Thornton was a leader of local opposition to the park's takeover of the Bull Creek canyon.

Your route, along what was once Thornton's road and beside what was once Albee's creek, continues along the flat until you reach a locked gate at 0.4 mile. Here the pavement ends and the road begins to climb very steeply, passing some water tanks and coming out onto a ridgeline. A prairie rises raggedly to the right, while the forested slope to the left drops towards the campground. California black oak, Oregon white oak, willow, and blueblossom grow at the roadside.

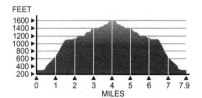

At 0.75 mile a side trail branches left. Bear right, soon crossing the hillside prairie, from which you can see the forested hump of Grasshopper Peak to the

southeast. You reenter the woods at 1.0 mile, with Albee Creek now below you to the right. Soon you regain and then recross the prairie, pass up the corridor of old Thornton Road, and then bend left into mixed second-growth forest. The trail now slackens its ascent, running almost levelly across the hillside. You cut across a very steep prairie at 1.75 miles that provides a vista southward of the old townsite of Bull Creek.

The trail returns to the woods, passing bigleaf maple and California bay and then crossing through a scattering of rocks and small boulders. After traversing another hillside prairie at 2.3 miles, the route again encounters mixed second-growth, making a switchback to the

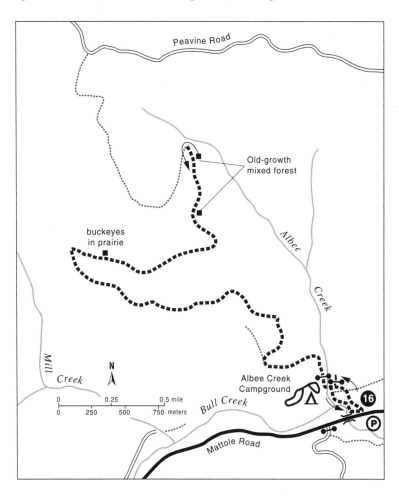

right at 2.6 miles as it nears the canyon of Mill Creek. You enter a higher section of the previous prairie at 2.85 miles. Look here for several California buckeyes at the prairie's edge.

California buckeye (*Aesculus californica*) is delightful to see, deadly to eat, and one of the most singular plants found in the parks. Of the five related species that grow in the U.S. (don't forget that Ohio is called the "Buckeye State") it is the only one native to California. Often the size of a large shrub, it can take on treelike proportions, with some buckeyes growing more than 40 feet tall. In spring it sends out striking spikes of pinkish white clustered flowers, but come mid- to late summer it astounds the unwary by dropping all of its deep green leaves. September sees the buckeye setting out numerous dark, leathery fruit capsules that dangle from its bare limbs like out-of-season Christmas ornaments. Every part of the buckeye is toxic to everything that might eat it—people, wildlife, and livestock. Indians would throw ground buckeye seed in the water, where it stunned

A prairie opening, Grasshopper Peak in distance

fish, which would then float to the surface and be easily caught. Buckeye wood, when dried in a kiln for several weeks, will develop a mottled green coloring akin to that of onyx. With characteristics such as these, it is not surprising that people keep their eyes on the California buckeye.

Leaving the prairie, the path again enters second-growth forest, reaching a ridge spur at 3.4 miles, which it crosses. The route resumes its course along the hillslope but now the surroundings are dramatically different. Evergreen huckleberry covers much of the forest floor. Large madrones are joined by medium-large Douglas-firs and redwoods, and then at 3.55 miles a North Coast rarity appears—mature tanoaks. The specimens usually seen today are spindly second-growth trees that form part of the forest understory, because most mature tanoaks were cut for their tannin-rich bark in the first half of the twentieth century. The tanbarkers swarmed over the Bull Creek countryside, but here, in one of the few spots they missed, old-growth tanoaks rise on magnificent, mossy trunks 150 feet and more, mixing with the madrones and conifers to create a few acres of ancient mixed forest. Adding to the effect at 3.7 miles is another collection of rocks and small boulders, many of them clothed in the same rich green moss that also decorates the madrones and tanoaks.

The trail passes a double-trunked redwood to the right, and then, nearing the canyon of Albee Creek, makes a switchback to the left. The elbow of the switchback points at a large double-trunked tanoak that seems to be mimicking the nearby redwood. Here the hike reverses course at mile 3.95, having reached its climax amid this patch of old-growth forest. You return to the Albee Creek bridge at 7.6 miles, whence you take a different route back to your starting point. Immediately after crossing the bridge, bear right onto a marked trail, soon dropping next to the shaded channel of Albee Creek. Presently the path bends left to run beside the larger waters of Bull Creek, which is screened by a ribbon of red alder. The trail meets a dirt access road at 7.75 miles, in front of a stream gauging station. Turn left onto the often muddy road and follow it 75 yards to Mattole Road, where you again turn left. Watch for traffic as you follow Mattole Road back to the campground entrance road, where the hike ends at 7.9 miles.

For a longer hike: Instead of turning back at 3.9 miles, continue on up Thornton Trail to where it ends at Peavine Road. Return from here to add 3.4 miles to the hike, for a total mileage of 11.3.

17. WHISKEY PRAIRIE

Features	■ fall forest colors and an oak-fringed prairie with views of Bull Creek
Distance	■ 3.7 miles round trip (longer option available)
Elevation gain	■ 550 feet
Difficulty	■ moderate
Open	■ all year

Driving directions: Drive to mile 6.2 of Mattole Road. Turn south onto the access road for Baxter Environmental Camp. Drive a few feet and park off the road before you reach a locked gate. The hike is on the Baxter Trail.

In the 1910s Bull Creek was known for its prize-winning apples. Then, during Prohibition, it developed a reputation for another commodity—bootleg whiskey, made at stills hidden in the area's secluded, heavily forested canyons. This hike takes you to an unnamed grassland that could well be called Whiskey Prairie, since one of the stills lay in the woods just south of it.

A steel gate blocks vehicular access to Baxter Environmental Camp, a small hike-in facility. Passing around the gate, you proceed southward on a gravel road. A willow thicket lies off to the right, while mixed forest covers the hillside to the left. Oregon ash, red alder, California bay, and bigleaf maple also line the roadside. At 0.2 mile the road ends in a turnaround at a second gate. Now the route follows a path that leads through the redwood-shaded camping area, named for Grace Johnson Baxter, a member of the pioneer Johnson ranching family. Baxter once had a home here. Just beyond a park outhouse, the trail divides. The way right provides access to a campsite, so you turn left. A short climb brings you to a junction at 0.3 mile. Right leads to a ford at Bull Creek, while your way is left. The wide pathway accommodates horses but you will probably encounter few of them—or hikers, either.

The trail ascends the hillside on a gentle grade, passing through second-growth conifers and a delightful mix of other trees. Many

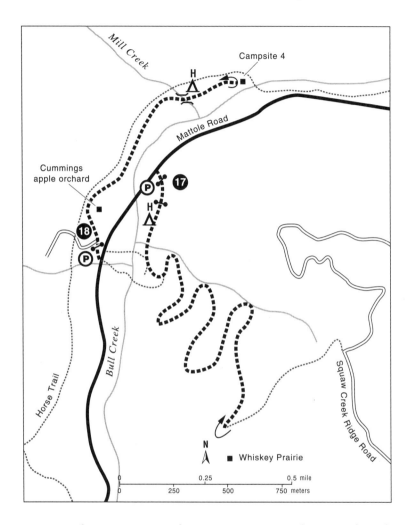

N
Λ ▪ Whiskey Prairie

years ago the area was part of a tie camp operation that cut redwoods into "bolts" several feet long. The bolts were then hand-hewed into "split products," including grape stakes, fence posts, and railroad ties. Various road remnants crisscross the trail.

Willow and Pacific dogwood appear at 0.65 mile. Then, after a switchback, come California bay, California hazel, and Pacific madrone, followed shortly by California black oak and more willow. In fall the woods come alive with color, the soft yellows and golds accented by glimpses of pale pink. After crossing a wooden bridge, the route runs past more hazel and then bigleaf maple. At 1.45 miles

Bull Creek Valley from Whiskey Prairie

you see tanoak, Douglas-fir, and evergreen huckleberry.

Watch closely for a switchback that cuts left at 1.8 miles. Leave the main trail here and follow the side path that leads directly off the elbow of the switchback. It runs south for some 200 feet, passing beneath bigleaf maple and Douglas-fir, to a large, steeply sloping prairie bordered by Oregon white oak. The view from the prairie encompasses, from right to left, Pole Line Road, the mouth of Cuneo Creek, and the Lewis apple orchard next to Bull Creek. Some conveniently placed fallen oak limbs allow you to sit and contemplate the view. The prairie drops in front of you all the way to Bull Creek, while to your left the grassland continues southeastward, cutting through a fringe of conifers and then continuing uphill until it reaches a forested stream canyon. One of Bull Creek's numerous stills was once hidden here, while over the ridgeline to the left is a spot called Whiskey Camp, where another still was cleverly concealed in a hollow redwood, the smoke from the still's fire issuing from the hole in the tree's top.

Although bootleg whiskey was always in high demand, the various distilling operations met with mixed success. Sometimes they would be discovered by other locals—one newcomer to the area ran across a still with a barrel containing twenty gallons of "fiery red liquid" whose fierce effects prevented him from sampling more than a small amount. Other times, as with the Whiskey Prairie operation, the "dry squad" located the still and the bootleggers were arrested. Times change, and eighty years later Bull Creek's illicit commodity has changed to marijuana, with cultivators locating secluded, well-watered sections of the canyon and then planting and maintaining small cannabis plots on state park property. The telltale wisp of still smoke has been replaced by the equally incriminating black plastic waterline that distinguishes the marijuana growers' agricultural technique.

From your oak "bench" at the edge of the prairie you return downhill by the same route to the trailhead.

For a longer hike: Continue uphill on the Baxter Trail, meeting Squaw Creek Ridge Road in 0.6 mile. Turn right here and take the road south, climbing gradually through redwoods until you reach the Whiskey Flat Trail Camp in an additional 1.9 miles. Turn back here and retrace your route to add 5 miles to your hike.

18. HAMILTON BARN

Features	▪	a prize-winning apple orchard and the site of a migrating lumber mill
Distance	▪	1.5 miles round trip
Elevation gain	▪	100 feet
Difficulty	▪	easy
Open	▪	all year

Driving directions: Drive to mile 6.5 of Mattole Road. Turn west onto the access road for the Hamilton Barn Environmental Camp. Drive a few feet and park off the road before you reach a locked gate.

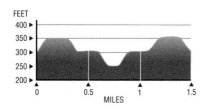

For about a century Bull Creek was a busy place, first with ranching, then with tanbark harvesting, and finally with logging. A dozen families lived here by the 1890s, while the post–World War II timber-cutting boom swelled the population to about three hundred. In the aftermath of the disastrous 1955 flood, when the Save-the-Redwoods League began buying up properties in the watershed and transferring them to the park, the town quickly began to shrink, and by the 1980s it was no more than a memory. This hike passes some of the landmarks of bygone Bull Creek.

Shaded parking for a couple of cars is available at the start of gravel-surfaced Hamilton Barn Road. (See map on page 83.) Be sure not to block access when you park. Notice the small stream that drops down a gulch to the left of the road—on the hilltop above it was once the Bull Creek School. Start uphill on the gravel road, soon passing around a gate. In another 100 feet a spur road forks to the left; ignore the spur and bear right. The road levels, passes a walnut tree to the right, and then a cluster of four Oregon ashes to the left. At 0.1 mile you come into an opening filled with apple trees. Early in the last century the orchard belonged to Amos Cummings, who in 1914 sent some of his King apples to a show in San Francisco, where they were regally received not with a crown but with a gold medal. The trees now show their age, having suffered from decades of neglect, but in spring you can still hope to see them white with blossoms that perfume the air.

The road enters forest and then drops downhill. Look for California bay, California hazel, and vanilla leaf at 0.3 mile. Soon the way levels, passing bigleaf maple and red alder before coming out into another open area. Coyote brush and blueblossom cover much of the opening. The road ends at 0.6 mile next to Mill Creek at a parking area for the Hamilton Barn Environmental Camp. In 1953 Hershell D. Wheeler decided to set up a logging mill here. He also decided to bring his mill machinery and workers from his last operation in Mississippi. One day a caravan of trucks arrived from half a continent away, and soon soft southern drawls were heard amid the shriek of Wheeler's mill saw. Wheeler and his crew drawled and sawed for nine years and two floods,

Opposite: Creek below old Bull Creek Schoolhouse

until the the mill burned. Wheeler sold his property to the park, and the banks of Mill Creek were silent once again.

A wooden bridge crosses the creek and leads through second-growth redwood to the start of the Hamilton Barn Environmental Camp. Turn right onto the trail for campsite 4, dropping to a small prairie that is bordered to the left by Oregon ash. At 0.7 mile a spreading bigleaf maple to the right shades part of the remains of the Hamilton homesite.

Ruby and Hugh Hamilton came to this spot on the bank above Bull Creek in 1910, having just been married *inside* a redwood. It was no more than a medium-size tree, so there was only room for the bride, groom, best man, bridesmaid, and minister. The rest of the party had to stand outside the "chapel." Hugh ranched on the property until his death, while Ruby stayed on until she had spent fifty-four years there. Then, like her neighbors in the valley, she sold out to the park and left. The ranch buildings, including the barn that gives the spot its name, were removed, and only a few fruit trees and flowers mark the spot.

The trail soon reaches campsite 4, situated just above the rippling waters of Bull Creek. If the site is not occupied, its table makes a nice location for lunch, after which you retrace your route, returning to its start at 1.5 miles.

19. POLE LINE ROAD

Features	▪	oak-fringed prairies, wide-ranging views, and the headwaters of Bear River
Distance	▪	4.8 miles round trip (longer hike option available)
Elevation gain	▪	1200 feet
Difficulty	▪	strenuous
Open	▪	all year (snow may cover the upper section of the hike in winter; check at the park visitor center for current conditions)

Driving directions: Drive to mile 7.3 of Mattole Road. The hike starts to the right on Pole Line Road.

The town of Bull Creek received its power from an electrical line that ran from the Rio Dell area over the mountains and down a long

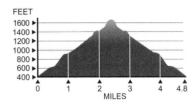

ridgeline to the town. The road that ran up the ridge next to the line became known as Pole Line Road. Today it is perhaps the most scenic way to climb to the ridge top from the valley of Bull Creek.

You begin the hike on gravel-surfaced Pole Line Road, which runs just above the waters of alder-shaded Cuneo Creek to the left. In 50 yards you pass a gate and begin climbing at the base of a wooded ridgeline. Coyote brush is followed by California

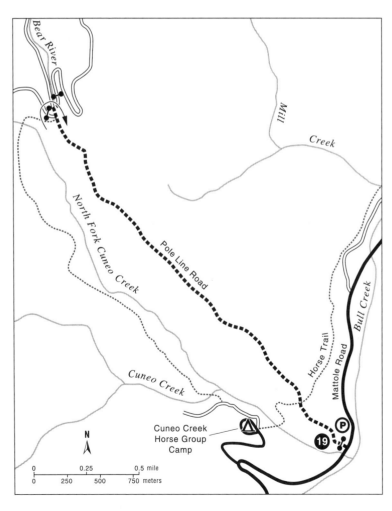

California black oak and clouds

bay, Oregon white oak, California black oak, and Douglas-fir. The road levels briefly and then resumes climbing. The Horse Trail, open to both equestrians and hikers, crosses at 0.3 mile. After rounding a bend, the road reaches a large prairie and then continues climbing next to its namesake power poles. In summer the prairie is dotted with California poppy and blue-eyed grass. You reenter woods at 0.7 mile and come to a second prairie. Directly ahead is a large California black oak, which you pass at 1.1 miles. Behind you is the looming bulk of Grasshopper Peak, and below it, conifer-covered Squaw Creek Ridge. To the west, across the canyon of the North Fork of Cuneo Creek, is a flat ridge top where John Cuneo once had part of his extensive orchard. After decades of neglect the fruit trees have been overtopped by encroaching conifers.

At 1.2 miles look on the right for a springtime scattering of daffodils. They cover part of an old homesite that lay next to the original Pole Line Road, which ran through the woods just behind the prairie. Your route returns to the forest, while the older road heads up the hillside to the right. California bay and Douglas-fir are prominent, and a bigleaf maple appears on your left at 1.6 miles. Nearby is blueblossom, which provides a sweet springtime scent.

Madrones line the roadside at 1.9 miles. Continuing to climb, you pass a pair of side roads to the right. Bend left, leaving the pole line, which runs up the hillside. A shaded ditch to the right is home to giant chain fern and seep-spring monkeyflower; California spikenard grows nearby. At 2.3 miles there are two junctions to the left. The first is with the Indian Orchard Trail, which drops downhill on its way to the Cuneo Creek Horse Camp. The second, immediately beyond the trail, is with Fox Camp Road, which winds and climbs to the ridgeline and eventually meets Mattole Road far to the southwest. You continue to the right, passing grand fir and Douglas-fir. After arriving at a junction with Peavine Road, turn right and proceed about 50 feet to the middle of an opening. To your left are the headwaters of Bear River, which descends into a deep canyon before emptying into the Pacific just west of the remote ghost town of Capetown. Here at its start are common cattail, Pacific Coast iris, and red flowering currant. Here, too, is where the route turns back, returning to nearby Pole Line Road and following it south to the trailhead at 4.8 miles.

For a longer hike: On your way back, take the Indian Orchard Trail, dropping into the canyon of North Fork Cuneo Creek, eventually crossing the west fork and then reaching the Cuneo Creek Horse Camp. From there take the Horse Trail eastward, dropping to cross Cuneo Creek and then climbing to reach Pole Line Road, where you turn right and descend a short distance to the trailhead. This alternate return adds 1.3 miles to your trip for a total mileage of 6.1. *Warning: this alternate return should not be attempted in winter, when heavy water flows make the Cuneo Creek crossing extremely dangerous.*

20. ALLENS

Features ■ a charming waterfall and a haunting hillside grove of redwoods
Distance ■ 2.8 miles round trip
Elevation gain ■ 1000 feet
Difficulty ■ strenuous
Open ■ all year

Driving directions: Drive to mile 22.1 (9.4) of the Avenue of the Giants. The trailhead is at a pullout on the western side of the road.

The most impressive stands of redwoods are usually found on the silt-rich flats near rivers and large creeks, but this hike leads you to a grove that is elevated in both altitude and quality, where the forest wraps you in stillness and the trees rise in solemn grandeur from the steep slopes.

The trailhead is to the right of a rocky gulch that splashes silver with the waters of winter and spring, but which may be dry come fall. The route begins climbing on switchbacks through mixed forest. Vanilla leaf and western trillium lie beneath a second story of sword fern and small tanoak, while conifers rise far overhead.

Tanoak (*Lithocarpus densiflorus*) is neither tan nor an oak, but it has proven to be one of the North Coast's most valued, and—when allowed to grow to majestic maturity—attractive trees. The tanoak is part of large genus of about three hundred species of trees and shrubs, but it is the only one native to California. All the rest reside in southeastern Asia and Indonesia. It was probably called an oak because it produces an acorn, one so tasty that the local Indians esteemed its edibility above those of all the true oaks. Whites found another use for the tree—which almost brought about its elimination, since tanoak bark is rich in the natural tannins once used by the leather industry to tan hides. For decades the hillsides of Humboldt were shorn of their cover of tanoak as the trees were felled and their bark stripped and sent to tanneries. Only with the introduction of synthetic tannins was the destruction stopped, and

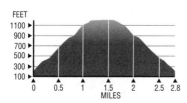

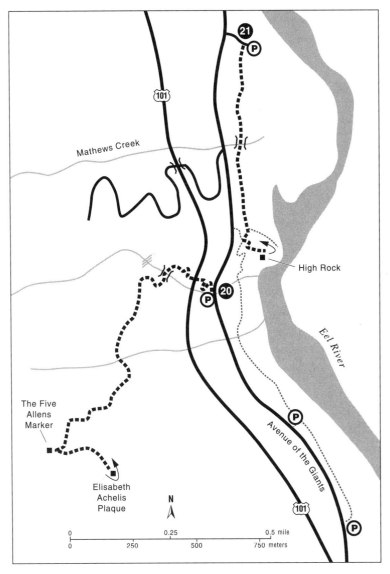

now most tanoaks are part of a generation of youngsters, often appearing as an understory plant. But find a stand of mature tanoaks and all this changes—the trees rise on stout, straight trunks as much as 200 feet tall—full-fledged members of the all-but-forgotten forest that once, before the time of the tanbarkers and the loggers, spread far and wide.

At 0.1 mile the trail passes beneath Highway 101 through a large

Coast redwood (left) and Douglas-fir (right)

culvert. Watch out for a festooning of poison oak that sometimes hangs from the entrance. More switchbacks then take you steeply upward, past milkmaids, until the route levels and bends into a small side canyon. Here, at 0.3 mile, a bridge crosses a mini waterfall. Benefiting from the moisture are five-finger fern, thimbleberry, California hazel, and, framing the approach to the bridge, western burning bush.

Now the trail resumes switchbacking, passing Pacific Coast iris at 0.7 mile and encountering a pair of large logs brightened by a covering of licorice fern at 1.05 miles. Salal and western trillium are found at the pathside. Presently you cross two creeklets that water vast numbers of sword ferns. Turn right at a junction and climb uphill about a 100 yards to the decaying wooden marker for The Five Allens, a quintet of quintessential conservationists. Return to the junction and turn right, crossing the slope past scatterings of salal before ending at the Elisabeth Achelis plaque at 1.4 miles. Here the landscape is of two lines: the steep diagonal of the green hillside, and the many gray verticals of the medium-large redwoods that rise from the sloping forest floor. The trees are numerous but spaced far enough apart to impart a feeling of openness. Green foliage softens the straight lines of the tree trunks, while a primeval quietness hangs in the air like a silencing fog. The array of redwoods continues into the distance, but there is a sense that the trail has come far enough, for few spots could provide such a calming, contemplative conclusion to the climb you've just experienced. *Pause here and you will refresh your spirit,* the grove seems to say, and it is difficult not to heed its whispered advice.

When you are ready to return, reverse course, bearing right at the only junction.

21. HIGH ROCK

Features ▪	a riverside redwood flat, a section of the old county wagon road, and a dramatic promontory above the Eel River
Distance ▪	1.2 miles round trip (longer option may be available)
Elevation gain ▪	200 feet
Difficulty ▪	moderate
Open ▪	all year

Driving directions: Drive to mile 22.8 (8.7) of the Avenue of the Giants. Turn east onto an unmarked, paved side road and drive 75 yards to a parking area at the end of the pavement. The trailhead is immediately to the southwest.

Before starting the hike, look skyward. Do you see a ladderlike construction high up in the large redwood at the southern edge of the parking area? This was the support framework for a pulley system used by the Mercer-Fraser Company, a Eureka construction firm, to remove gravel from the nearby riverbar. Now, looking trailward, begin the hike, passing redwood sorrel, poison oak, and thin false Solomon's seal while walking beneath large redwoods. (See map on page 93.) Notice a thicket of dark green, leafy shoots on the right at mile 0.1. This is cestrum, a tropical shrub also known as bastard jasmine, which has somehow managed to survive in the shadows of a northern California forest.

Watch for encroaching poison oak as you pass several grove markers. A railed bridge spans a small chasm at 0.25 mile, offering a view of the exposed alluvium that composes the walls of the gorge. After passing the Wentworth Grove, you begin to ascend the hillside, at times following sections of the county wagon road that preceded the Redwood Highway.

A scattering of vanilla leaf at the trailside is followed by a spur trail to the left that leads down to the nearby Eel River. Bear right, continuing uphill and passing another spur trail to the right that connects to a parking area on the Avenue. A switchback then takes you to another junction at 0.55

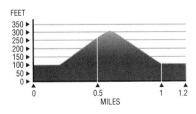

mile. Turn left here, leaving the main trail, and climb uphill on switchbacks past Hooker's fairybell and fat false Solomon's seal.

Thin false Solomon's seal (*Smilacina stellate* var. *sessifolia*) and fat false Solomon's seal (*Smilacina racemosa* var. *amplexicaulis*) are related but vastly different in appearance and habitat. Although both grow in redwood forests, the thin species prefers the level ground of benchlands, while the fat likes to sprout from hillsides and roadcuts. The thin has long stiletto-shaped leaves and a small collection of individual starlike flowers. The fat has wider, more robust leaves, and its stem culminates in a cluster of tiny white flowers that provide the sweetest of scents. After blooming, the fat species produces a group of berries, speckled at first and then growing deep red. Though as Solomon's seals both plants may be false, in other respects they are *truly* a delight.

The trail then comes out onto the top of High Rock, known to the local Lolahnkok Indians as *Sa'cho'te*. Two sections of railings on your right mark the top of a steep cliff that drops riverward. The Eel is best seen from the overlook at the end of the trail at 0.6 mile. The cliffside is adorned with several striking plants, including canyon live oak, toyon, hound's tongue, orange bush monkeyflower, and Indian warrior.

After contemplating the various views, retrace your steps to the trailhead, arriving there at 1.2 miles.

For a longer hike: If the main trail is open south of the High

Fat false Solomon's seal in fruit

Rock turnoff, continue on it, dropping down to another flat and crossing two long bridges before reaching the Avenue at 1.2 miles, whence you retrace your route, adding 1.2 miles to the hike. *Note: At the time of publication this section of trail was closed due to a damaged bridge. Check at the park visitor center for current status.*

22. FRENCH GROVE LOOPS

Features	■ a charming miniature forest landscape and the historic Girdled Tree
Distance	■ 0.75 mile, two loops
Elevation gain	■ negligible
Difficulty	■ easy
Open	■ all year

Driving Directions: Drive to mile 28.6 (2.9) of the Avenue of the Giants, just south of Pepperwood. The trailhead is on the western side of the road. *Warning: Poison oak loves to encroach on the edges of this lovely trail. Watch closely for its three-leaved clusters near the path.*

Few other spots in the redwoods, if any, are as delicately beautiful as the French Grove. And no other location can offer anything remotely like the Girdled Tree, which has survived for a century in spite of losing much of its lower bark. You can treat your eyes and soothe your spirit with less than a mile of walking, and the memory will likely last forever.

The hike begins at a pullout on the west side of the Avenue, where a sign indicates access to the Greig, French, and Bell groves. Several of the first redwoods you pass bear a strange band of discoloration on their trunks—a faded grayish or yellowish tint that rises from ground level some 15 feet high. The bands mark Pepperwood's most memorable event, the 1964 flood.

During Christmas week of 1955, a devastating storm swept through Humboldt County. Its runoff ran so high that it was labeled the "hundred-year" flood. When an even bigger storm hit nine years to the day later in 1964, there was only one thing to call its result: the "thousand-year" flood. Towns

throughout the region were devastated, and Pepperwood was among the hardest hit. Rancher Henry Millsap evacuated his home, then thought better of it, and with his grandson, John Hower, rowed back to the house. They arrived just in time to see the floodwaters lift the building from its foundation and begin to move it downriver. Millsap and Hower immediately rowed after their runaway house, caught up with it, and succeeded in rescuing family belongings from the attic before the structure was finally swept away. Others fared worse. Five refugees trapped on the second floor of the Tower Auto Court drowned in the rising floodwaters before a helicopter could be dispatched to rescue them. At the end, Pepperwood was nothing but a mass of wrecked houses piled upon one another and mixed with jumbles of logs and other debris. Two great floods in fewer than ten years were too much for most residents, and the town was never rebuilt.

Past the grove sign the trail bears left, passing poison oak, smooth yellow violet, thin false Solomon's seal, and other forest plants that repose in the shadows of large redwoods. After cutting through a thicket of lady fern, the path reaches a Lilliputian landscape—a carpet of cloverlike redwood sorrel covers both the ground and fallen logs like thousands of trees in some tiny forest. Here and there a smooth yellow violet or some other larger flower rises a few inches higher to tower over the deep green sorrel. Narrow side paths lead off invitingly to the left, while the main trail makes its way to the historic Girdled Tree at 0.2 mile. This 50-foot-circumference redwood had a large section of its lower bark removed in 1901 by members of the

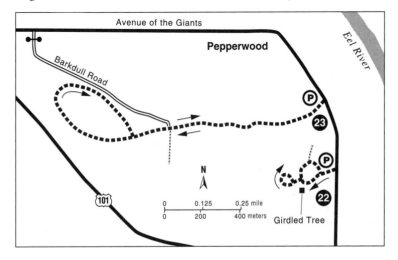

Girdled Tree

French family. The bark was then taken to San Francisco and used for a convention display. Despite the loss of much of its lower covering, the Girdled Tree has survived for another hundred-plus years and appears ready to continue for a few centuries more.

Just ahead the trail reaches what the authors call "the French bench," dedicated to one of the French sons, Percy, and his wife. Years after his girdling work, Percy became the first superintendent of the local state park district. Turn left here at a fork, soon reaching the southern edge of the grove, which is bordered by a dark stand of second-growth trees. The trail continues on to the short Winifred Brown Bell Grove loop, after which you return to the French bench at 0.6 mile. Turn left here and take a narrow path though an understory of coast red elderberry, California bay, and bigleaf maple. At the far end of a fallen redwood, the trail forks; turn right on yet a narrower route, crossing between two sections of a large log and then meeting the first part of the trail at 0.7 mile. Turn left to regain the Avenue.

23. DRURY-CHANEY GROVES LOOP

Features ▪	large redwoods and small pepperwoods
Distance ▪	2.45 miles round trip with loop (longer options available)
Elevation gain ▪	negligible
Difficulty ▪	moderate
Open ▪	all year

Driving Directions: Drive to mile 28.8 (2.7) of the Avenue of the Giants, immediately south of Pepperwood. The trailhead is on the western side of the road.

This lovely loop honors two leaders in the Save-the-Redwoods League. Newton B. Drury was both the League's first secretary and its third—he left for nineteen years to direct first the National Park Service and then the California Division of Beaches and Parks while his brother Aubrey took over running the League. Upon Aubrey's death, Newton returned as executive secretary, which meant that one Drury or another led the organization for all of its first fifty-two years. Ralph W. Chaney, a paleontologist at the University of California at Berkeley, was president of the League from 1961 to 1971. In 1948 he journeyed to a remote village in central China, where a species of redwood previously thought to be

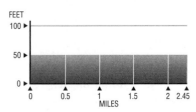

California bay (pepperwood)

extinct had recently been discovered. After a perilous trip that included an attack by bandits, Chaney was able to obtain some "dawn" redwood seedlings, which he brought back to the United States. Later Chaney and others distributed baby dawn redwoods to many locations, so that today they are found growing on three continents. One is in front of the visitor center at Humboldt Redwoods State Park; another is at the side of the Eureka City Hall. Yet another is located in—of all places—Cleveland, Ohio.

The trail crosses through a patch of grass before reaching the Chaney plaque. (See map on page 98.) There you plunge into a wall of greenery, twisting through a forest filled with redwood sorrel, large logs, sword fern, and many spindly California bays *(Umbellularia californica)*. The latter are sometimes called pepperwood, and it was their presence that gave the nearby town its name. The mature trees are stout-trunked masses of aromatic, dark green leaves, but here all you see is second growth, some so frail that they bend over in a wide arc, their tops nearly touching the ground. During World War I, bays were in great demand for shipbuilding, their straight trunks used for masts or for interior paneling. By the end of the war, almost all the trees had been cut, and what you see now is only a haunting whisper of what once filled the flats of Pepperwood.

At 0.6 mile the path arrives at Barkdull Road. A few hundred yards to the left this historic route reaches the site of the Barkdull Ranch, whose Travellers Inn served as a stopping place a century ago. Across the road, the trail continues in redwoods, reaching a junction at 0.75 mile where the two ends of the loop portion of the trail meet. Go left, soon passing a patch of false lily-of-the-valley and a thicket of California hazel. The trail winds through the redwoods, crossing a barely moving creeklet at 1 mile. The ground here contains gourmet-quality food for the surrounding forest, for the Pepperwood area is located upon one of several benchlands along the lower Eel that are filled with nutrient-rich alluvium. These deposits of silt, gravel, and other materials have been washed down the river over millennia and have lodged at various locations, including here. The fertile soil that you tread upon has produced more than world-class redwoods—luscious Pepperwood tomatoes, grown nearby, were once shipped by train to much of California and even to Nevada.

You then encounter two spur trails on the left that lead a few feet along the benchland to memorial grove benches, after which you reach the end of the loop at 1.7 miles. Turn left, soon recrossing Barkdull Road and arriving back at the trailhead at 2.45 miles.

For a longer hike: You can turn either direction at Barkdull Road. The way left leads to an opening where the old ranch was situated, and a trip there and back adds 0.8 mile to the trip. Going right takes you through more of Pepperwood's great redwood forest before arriving at the Avenue of the Giants west of town. This route also adds 0.8 mile to the hike.

24. OLD HIGHWAY 101 SOUTH

Features	▪ a haunting section of abandoned highway and a maple-shaded concrete bridge
Distance	▪ 0.6 mile round trip
Elevation gain	▪ negligible
Difficulty	▪ easy
Open	▪ all year

Driving directions: Drive to mile 31.4 (0.1) of the Avenue of the Giants. Turn northwest onto Elinor Road and drive 150 yards to a concrete barricade where the road makes a right turn. Park in front of the barricade, being careful not to block Elinor Road. The hike starts at the right side of the barricade.

The Redwood Highway was built through Eel River country in the 1910s. Two decades later it was upgraded to meet more modern standards. Then, in the 1960s, the section from Garberville to Rio Dell was replaced by freeway, and over 30 miles of the old highway became a scenic alternate known as the Avenue of the Giants. When the northern end of the Avenue was connected to the new freeway, this short section of the old highway was abandoned. Now its pavement is obscured by a cover of redwood needles and hikers have replaced the Studebakers, Packards, and other bygone vehicles that once passed along it. Here, by walking westward about a quarter mile in the forest, you can travel much farther in a different direction—back in time some six or seven decades.

Passing around the barricade, you follow the wide corridor of the old highway past bigleaf maples and big-trunked redwoods. You soon cross between sections of a fallen redwood and then pass a hollow stump to the right that rests invitingly on its side. The route then detours to the right to bend around another large log before returning to the roadway. If you scuff the duff with your boot, you'll probably find pavement underneath, or, if you're especially lucky, a faded stripe of white line. Redwood sorrel borders the way, while California hazel, poison oak, and bigleaf maple provide dazzling fall color. The

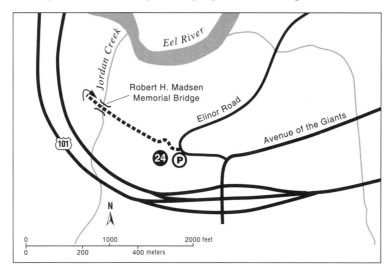

corridor here is more open, allowing nearly unobstructed views of entire redwoods—a rare opportunity since most of the tall trees are packed close together in roadless groves.

At 0.25 mile an aging concrete bridge spans the rocky bed of Jordan Creek. The date "1938" is engraved on the facings at the start of both railings. Bigleaf maples extend long, low-slung limbs over the bridge in a seeming attempt to become part of the architecture. A sign indicates that the structure is now called the Robert H. Madsen Memorial Bridge. It wasn't called that when Madsen, then a college student, was helping to build the bridge for the Depression-era wage of a penny a minute. It is well worth pausing for at least a dime's worth of time to contemplate what Madsen helped create: the concrete span sweeps gracefully across the creek, the balustrades on either side providing both a sense of stoutness and a grille-like decorative effect. Perhaps in its abandonment the bridge has at last found its final purpose—a fixture in a fleeting world, where one can pause, and then linger, and finally realize that a bridge can connect both place *and* time.

The roadway continues across the bridge to mile 0.3, where it becomes obscured by vegetation, including more poison oak. Turn back here, watching for the many licorice ferns that grow upon the duff-covered pavement and also for further top-to-bottom views of redwoods. The hike concludes at the parking area at 0.6 mile.

Walk-through log next to old highway

REDWOOD NATIONAL PARK

Born amid controversy after decades of unfulfilled hopes, Redwood National Park has since its start been inextricably linked with the three northernmost state redwood parks, combining with them to protect a collection of old-growth forestlands unequaled by any except those of Humboldt Redwoods to the south. The lands of the national park, which were acquired more than forty years after the neighboring state parks got their starts, complement and connect the redwood tracts found at Prairie Creek, Del Norte Coast, and Jedediah Smith, so that the four parks together now comprise more than 130,000 acres of diverse and scenic landscape, of which 38,982 acres are ancient redwoods.

By the 1960s it was clear that the days of great tracts of redwood forestland were numbered. As improvements in logging technology combined with the North Coast timber industry's voracious appetite, acre after acre of old-growth fell before the whine of chain saws and the roar of log-laden trucks. Although substantial stands of magnificent redwoods had already been protected in state parks, preservationists still hoped for the creation of a national redwood park that would contain the best of the remaining forestland. But the tree-savers faced both external and internal conflict. Local opposition to a national redwood park—outspoken and strong—was led by lumber company owners who warned of a "lockup" of timber lands; they were dutifully followed by their workers, who feared the loss of their jobs. Compounding the problem, there was a lack of agreement among the preservationists. The Save-the-Redwoods League favored a park centered on Mill Creek, between the existing Jedediah Smith and Del Norte Coast State Parks, while the Sierra Club wanted a park that featured the Tall Trees Grove on Redwood Creek. Despite these difficulties, the time for Redwood National Park had come, and after much political maneuvering and appeasement, President Lyndon B. Johnson signed the enabling legislation on October 2, 1968.

But, as earlier happened with Humboldt Redwoods to the south, the effects of continued logging upstream placed old-growth parkland at risk. In this case, the newly shorn slopes above Redwood Creek discharged their silt and gravel into the streambed, where the aggressive alluvium threatened the redwoods at the Tall Trees Grove. More controversy ensued, but again the preservationists prevailed and a 48,000-acre park expansion act was signed by President Jimmy Carter in 1978. Included was much of the cutover Redwood Creek watershed directly upstream from the tall trees.

Nowadays, the California and federal parklands are operated cooperatively as Redwood National and State Parks, with separate staffs and facilities but with coordinated services and programs. For the purposes of this guidebook we have divided Redwood National Park into three sections, each of which alternates, as you move up the coast, with one of the state parks. From south to north, these are:

Orick to Prairie Creek: This section starts at Redwood National Park's southern boundary and includes the Kuchel Information Center south of Orick, Redwood Creek, the Bald Hills, and areas near the southern end of Prairie Creek, including Skunk Cabbage and Lost Man Creeks.

Prairie Creek to Del Norte Coast: Included here are areas on both sides of the mouth of the Klamath River, along with the strip of

Banana slug

coastline running north to Wilson Creek. The park has no information centers in this area.

Del Norte Coast to Jedediah Smith Redwoods State Park: Starting at Nickel Creek, this section runs up the coast and then onto the ridge between Highway 101 and Mill Creek. It also includes the Little Bald Hills, east of Jedediah Smith. Redwood National Park has two information centers nearby, one in downtown Crescent City and the other at Hiouchi, across Highway 199 from the Jed Smith campground. For a list of park facilities, see the appendix.

Some of the most diverse hikes in this book are contained in these three sections of Redwood National Park. Two hikes in the Bald Hills take you through historic sheep ranching country set in a mix of oak woodlands and prairies. Two hikes acquaint you with old mill sites, where the one-time mill ponds teem with plants and wildlife. Five hikes feature ocean views and/or stretches of beach. And a few, as you might expect, take you into redwood forest.

ORICK TO PRAIRIE CREEK

25. REDWOOD CREEK

Features	▪	beautiful bigleaf maples, an elk-inhabited meadow, and rock-strewn Redwood Creek
Distance	▪	3.2 miles round trip (longer option available in summer)
Elevation gain	▪	negligible
Difficulty	▪	moderate
Open	▪	all year for the basic hike

Driving directions: Take Highway 101 to Bald Hills Road, 1.3 miles north of downtown Orick. Proceed east on Bald Hills Road for 0.4 mile and then turn right onto a paved access road for the Redwood Creek Trail. Take this road 0.5 mile to a parking area at the trailhead.

In the 1940s and 1950s the parking lot was home to the Orick Lumber Company, whose mill incorporated the boiler from the steam schooner *Yellowstone*, which had wrecked in 1933 while attempting to enter Humboldt Bay. Fortunately, whatever cutting the company did failed to include the hillside southeast of the mill, where an 8000-acre stretch of old-growth redwoods runs above Redwood Creek, constituting one of the largest stands of ancient forest found in any of the redwood parks.

The full Redwood Creek Trail travels some 8-plus miles to the Tall Trees Grove—a trip there and back is more than a day's worth of hiking. As a result, this hike goes only as far as the first creek crossing, but along the way it showcases its full share of scenery.

A bridge at the southeastern edge of the parking lot marks the start of the trail, which follows a broad track beneath red alder and bigleaf maple. In spring the trailside often displays the burgundy (or occasionally yellow) flowers of the giant trillium (*Trillium chloropetalum*), a cousin of the western trillium (*Trillium ovatum*), whose white flowers frequently

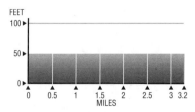

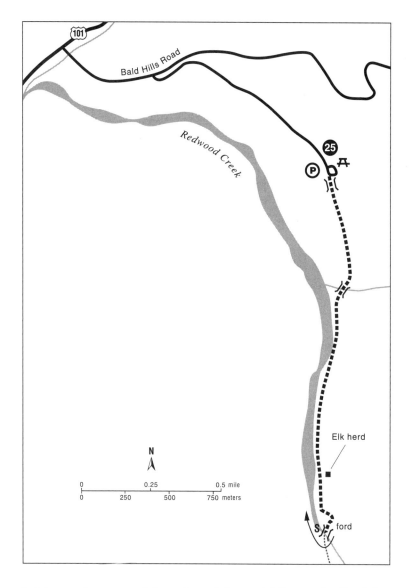

brighten other parts of the redwood forest. Adding to the floral display is a pair of small but striking plants, western bleeding heart and milkmaids.

The trail runs close to the left-hand hillside, while Redwood Creek makes its course beyond the alders to the right. Just past a bridge at 0.35 mile a magnificent, mossy-limbed bigleaf maple rises from the

Elk herd at trailside

left of the trail like a living, leafy monument, its supple contortions exhibiting an artistry that no sculptor could hope to achieve.

At 0.7 mile the trail turns right, moving into a prairie filled with blackberry bushes. Bridges span small streamlets that feed into Redwood Creek, which lies some 50 yards to the right. A view across the creek at 1.15 miles shows a band of gray-barked alders dwarfed by the dark trunks and foliage of the redwoods that rise behind them.

Red alder (*Alnus rubra*) is a commonly found colonizer of damp, open places, often filling the voids created by clearcuts. Alders are themselves cut commercially, being used for tool handles, furniture, and pulp products. The tree serves several purposes for the local Indians: its wood's aromatic smoke is used for curing salmon; its roots become a weaving thread for their baskets; and its bark produces a burnt orange dye that fades to deep brown. If left alone, red alder has an additional value—its roots contain nitrogen-fixing bacteria that improve soil quality. Less practical but also important is the aesthetic effect created by a stand of slender, pale-barked trees, their trunks swaying gracefully in the breeze, their leaves rustling gently as they rub against one another in close companionship. Their proximity to the dark, stout conifers creates a pleasing contrast for all who are fortunate enough to observe it.

An opening to the left at 1.3 miles is often occupied by Redwood Creek's resident elk herd. Soon the trail reenters forest, winding its way past more giant trilliums and passing a licorice-fern-covered snag on the right before dropping to the gravelly bank of the creek at 1.6 miles. On the far side is an osprey nest in the dead top of a large redwood. Here the route reverses course to the parking lot at 3.2 miles.

For a longer hike: In summer, cross Redwood Creek on the seasonal bridge and continue upstream; the trail recrosses the creek 7 miles ahead and ends at the Tall Trees Grove, which makes for a very long (17-mile) round-trip day hike. The route is lined with many scenic spots, any of which would make a good turnaround point.

26. LADY BIRD JOHNSON GROVE LOOP

Features	▪	a ridge-top grove of redwoods and the dedication site for Redwood National Park
Distance	▪	1.3 miles, loop
Elevation gain	▪	100 feet
Difficulty	▪	easy
Open	▪	all year, unless snow prevents access (check with a Redwood National Park information center for current status of Bald Hills Road)

Driving directions: Take Highway 101 to Bald Hills Road, 1.3 miles north of downtown Orick. Turn east onto Bald Hills Road and drive 2.7 miles to the trailhead parking lot on the right.

President Lyndon B. Johnson signed the bill authorizing the creation of Redwood National Park in 1968. His wife, Lady Bird, officiated at the dedication of the park. In 1969 the newly elected president, Richard M. Nixon, dedicated this grove to Lady Bird. Attending the ceremony, in addition to Johnson and Nixon, was someone who would later join their ranks, the then-governor of California, Ronald Reagan.

The trail leaves the west end of the parking area, immediately ascending a wood and concrete viaduct that spans Bald Hills Road. A box for trail guide brochures sits

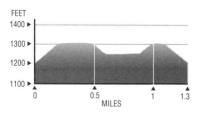

100 yards up the trail on the right. The forest here is a combination of redwood and Douglas-fir, with Pacific rhododendron, evergreen huckleberry, and salal underneath.

At 0.2 mile the trail forks. Bear left to begin the loop portion of the route. The path is broad; in this section it is built on the bed of the original Bald Hills Road, the berm of which can be seen at the trailside at 0.4 mile. In earlier days horse-drawn wagons and stages would climb the "four-mile mountain" from the flats north of Orick, coming out onto a long ridgeline that led southeastward into a region of oak woodlands and prairies known as the Bald Hills. Several ranches were strung out along the road, including that of the Tomlinson family, near Schoolhouse Peak, which served as an overnight stopping place for travelers on their way to Orleans and other points east. A 10-foot-long woodstove in the Tomlinsons' kitchen featured a griddle capable of frying twenty-five flapjacks at a time. The stove also served to boil the

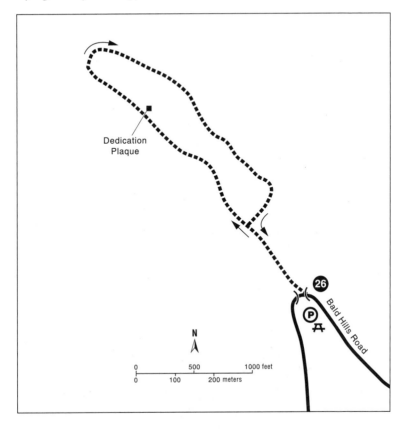

Trail viaduct over Bald Hills Road

bed sheets, all fifty of which had to be scrubbed by hand. When logging in the Redwood Creek and Klamath River drainages accelerated after World War II, the narrow road, with its 23 percent grade up the hillside, proved incapable of accommodating the resultant traffic, and so the current road was constructed in the 1950s.

Now the trail drops gently to reach the grove's dedication plaque at 0.5 mile. A short distance ahead, the route bends sharply right, leaving the old roadbed, and turns eastward, soon to run along a redwood-rich hillside. Fat false Solomon's seal, vanilla leaf, and deer fern line the way. The path crosses between two sections of a 5-foot-diameter log and then completes its loop at 1.1 miles. You turn left here and return to the parking area.

27. DOLASON PRAIRIE

Features	▪	a hillside ramble high above Redwood Creek and an oddly shaped sheep shed
Distance	▪	2.6 miles round trip (longer options available)
Elevation gain	▪	400 feet
Difficulty	▪	strenuous
Open	▪	all year, except when rendered inaccessible and impassable due to snow (if in doubt, check at a Redwood National Park information center for current status)

Driving directions: Take Highway 101 to Bald Hills Road, 1.3 miles north of downtown Orick. Turn east on Bald Hills Road

113

and follow it 11.4 miles to the access road on the right. Take the access road a few yards to the parking lot. *Note: This hike can be hot and sunny. Be sure to bring protective clothing and plenty of liquids; also be aware that the grassy areas off the trail are havens for ticks. Note also that Bald Hills Road is paved for its first 10 miles, after which it gradually turns to gravel.*

During the 1860s James Donaldson ranched on a prairie in the Bald Hills. The prairie took his name, sort of, but the spelling was corrupted into Dolason. In 1914, when Sherman Lyons owned the property, he built a 60-foot-square sheep shed on the grassy hillside, but, like the prairie, it has become misnamed, and has long been called a "barn." Adding to the building's indignity, it later had a portion of one side removed, so that it now has, architecturally speaking, a "saltbox" shape. In any case, the structure and its surrounding prairie, situated above the forested Redwood Creek Canyon, constitute one of the most scenic sites in the Bald Hills and are an ample reward for hikers who choose to make the trip.

The trailhead is at the southern edge of the forest-shaded parking lot. The route immediately emerges into the open and bends left to descend southeastward through prairie. A band of dark green forest covers the hillside across the canyon. Soon the route enters its own forest, passing a Douglas-fir at 0.2 mile, whose huge lower limbs indicate that it is a "wolf" tree. Such specimens developed at a time when the surrounding area was open, which allowed the wolf (as in lone) tree's uninhibited limbs to grow exuberantly. In recent years, young trees have encroached on the prairie so that the once-solitary wolf has become part of an ever-growing pack.

Presently the path switchbacks to the right and picks up an old roadbed, which it follows until reentering the prairie at 0.35 mile. Soon the route meets what was once known as the K and K Road, a wide thoroughfare that once served as a log-truck freeway for the Simpson Timber Company. The road connected Simpson mills at Korbel (K #1) and Klamath (K #2). Turn right and follow the roadway through an

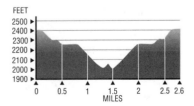

oak-dappled prairie until mile 0.75, where, just opposite an aging K and K sign, the trail drops to the left. The route first runs beneath Douglas-fir and then, after picking up another old roadbed, encounters tanoak and California

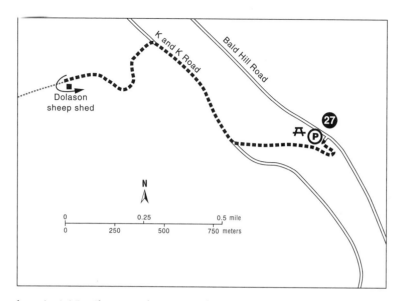

bay. At 1.05 miles a creek crossing finds bigleaf maple shading piggy-back plant and western wild ginger.

The route enters Dolason Prairie at 1.2 miles and comes to the barn/sheep shed. The first view is of the truncated side, which has been covered over with corrugated galvanized sheeting. The structure sits upon the prairie like a sharp-angled, out-of-balance sculpture. The eye searches for another object to put the building in perspective, but there is only the distant, dark green ridgeline and the nearby tawny grass gently bending in the breeze. The Dolason sheep shed stands alone upon the landscape, while around it the afternoon wind whispers of the vanished sheep ranches for all who choose to listen. The route reverses direction here, reaching the trailhead at 2.6 miles.

For a longer hike: You can continue down the Dolason Prairie Trail, eventually entering thick forest and crossing sublime Emerald Creek 3.4 miles ahead. Returning from this point creates a hike 9.4 miles in total length, with a 2200-foot elevation gain. If that seems too daunting, you can either turn back earlier, or, if you've arranged a car shuttle, continue on 0.2 additional mile to the Emerald Creek Trail, turn right on it, and hike 1 mile to reach your shuttle car at the Tall Trees parking area. If you choose this latter option, you can extend it farther by hiking the Tall Trees Trail down and back from the parking area. For information about car access to the Tall Trees trailhead, contact a Redwood National Park information center.

Dolason Prairie and Dolason sheep shed

28. LYONS RANCH LOOP

Features	■ picturesque old ranch buildings, cascading oak woodlands, and a rare wildflower hybrid
Distance	■ 4.65 miles, loop
Elevation gain	■ 450 feet
Difficulty	■ strenuous
Open	■ spring, summer, and fall (snow can prevent access in cold weather—check with a Redwood National Park visitor center for current conditions)

Driving directions: Take Highway 101 to Bald Hills Road, 1.3 miles north of downtown Orick. Turn east on Bald Hills Road and follow it 17 miles to the access road to the Lyons Ranch Trail on the right. Turn onto the access road and drive 100 yards to the parking area.

Note: This hike can be hot and sunny. Be sure to bring protective clothing and plenty of liquids; also be aware that the grassy areas off the trail are havens for

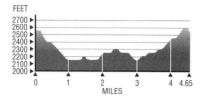

FEET
2700 ►
2600 ►
2500 ►
2400 ►
2300 ►
2200 ►
2100 ►
2000 ►
0   1   2   3   4 4.65
MILES

*ticks. Note also that Bald Hills Road
is paved for its first 10 miles, after
which it gradually turns to gravel.*

Want a change from the cool
coast and its redwood forests?
Try this hike in the oak woodlands above Redwood Creek, and
you'll get to visit a historic ranch site to boot.

The Bald Hills, which form the ridgeline northeast of Redwood
Creek, were once home to the Chilula Indians and to vast herds of
Roosevelt elk. A century and a half ago whites came to the area, killed
off the elk, and restocked the "balds"—grassy prairies fringed by oaks—
with range cattle. For a time the Chilulas resisted, at one point driving out all the ranchers and burning every one of their buildings, but
in 1864 the violence ended with the signing of a treaty that established the Hoopa Valley Indian Reservation. The Chilulas moved onto
the reservation, new ranchers arrived—first with cattle, later with
sheep—and eventually much of the area became part of Redwood
National Park. The park immediately began rehabilitating the area,
which had not only long been ranched but also heavily logged. Today,
herds of elk again roam the hillsides, while vestiges of the Bald Hills'
largest ranching operation are preserved by the park.

The hike begins by passing around a metal gate that blocks the

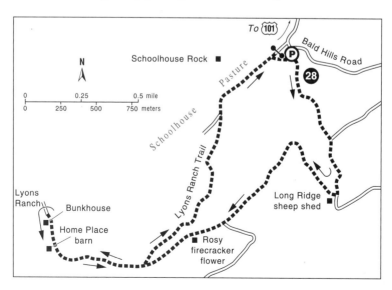

Lyons Ranch Trail, which is actually a well-maintained dirt road. Immediately past the gate, turn left onto a lesser-used road and begin dropping across a grass-covered hillslope. At 0.2 mile begin looking for spring-blooming Ithuriel's spear and hayfield tarweed. A rocky creek gorge at 0.35 mile is shaded by Oregon white oak and filled with both poison oak and poison delphinium. The latter, a tall plant with a spike of beautiful deep blue-violet flowers, is deadly to cattle. The route then passes a side road to the left that leads upward to Bald Hills Road. Continue downhill to the right. Watch for elk.

The road then switchbacks as it continues downhill, reaching a large metal-roofed structure shaped like an inverted V at 0.9 mile. This is the Long Ridge sheep shed, which is often mistaken by the uninformed for a barn. In winter, sheep would be fed inside this mostly open-sided building—one aging photo shows 1630 of the ravenous ruminants plodding through the snow to reach their long-awaited dinner in the shed.

Here the road forks; turn right, passing between the front of the shed and a rusting trailer that no doubt once housed one of the ranch's shepherds. The route cuts laterally across the hillside, passing through woodlands that feature both California black and Oregon white oak. At

Looking down on Schoolhouse Pasture

1.9 miles the road bends around a large madrone to the right and comes to a small pullout on the left. In midsummer this open space is home to a seldom-seen hybrid plant called the rosy firecracker flower (*Dichelostemma ida-maia x congestum*), which results from the cross pollination of the "regular" firecracker flower (*Dichelostemma ida-maia*) and forktooth ookow (*Dichelostemma congestum*). All three flowers can be seen here growing within a few feet of each other. Each is spectacular in its own right, but seen together they form an especially intriguing trio.

A short climb brings you into prairie at 2.25 miles, where you meet the road called Lyons Ranch Trail. Turn left, dropping gently along the hillside as views of the Redwood Creek drainage open to the left. Visible across the canyon is the two-tone-green patchwork that reveals the location of several large, rectangular clearcuts done before the redwood-rich land became part of the park. Closer at hand are scatterings of the state flower, the California poppy, which in this area is lemon yellow, a sharp contrast to the orange California poppy that so often embellishes North Coast highways but whose true home is in the southern part of the state.

After rounding a bend at 2.75 miles the Lyons's Home Place Barn appears on the left. Continue a short distance along the road into a wooded canyon, passing a decaying bunkhouse on the left. Just ahead, also on the left, was the last Lyons ranch house.

Jonathan and Amelia Lyons settled on the property in the late 1860s, added children and acreage, and eventually four Lyons family ranches stretched across 10 miles of the Bald Hills. With the ranches of their sons strung out to the west, the original ranch became known as the Home Place. Although the barn has survived for more than a century, the first three ranch houses all burned, and the fourth, a more modern structure, was removed by the park.

Here you reverse course, ascending to the junction with the road to Long Ridge at 3.55 miles. Bear left, continuing uphill on the Lyons Ranch Trail. A shaded creek canyon is filled with vegetation, including several plants, such as western trillium and Smith's fairybell, more commonly seen in the redwood forest.

You continue to climb through a mix of woodlands and prairie. At 4.3 miles ignore a side road to the left. Crest the ridge and drop slightly into the saddle of Schoolhouse Pasture. Schoolhouse Rock looms darkly to the left, while Schoolhouse Peak rises directly ahead. Of the schoolhouse itself, no sign remains. You then arrive at the gate and the end of the hike at 4.65 miles.

29. SKUNK CABBAGE CREEK

Features ▪	giant Sitka spruce and a stream canyon filled with skunk cabbage
Distance ▪	2.8 miles round trip (longer option available)
Elevation change ▪	negligible
Difficulty ▪	easy
Open ▪	year round

Driving directions: Take Highway 101 to the access road for the Skunk Cabbage Section, Coastal Trail, 1.7 miles north of downtown Orick. Turn west on the access road and drive on pavement 0.1 mile to a junction with a private road on the left. Bear right, following a gravel park road for 0.6 mile to its end at the trailhead.

Few routes in the redwoods are at their best in early March, but this trail is an exception. It is then that the shaded stream canyon through which it runs is brightened by the vivid yellow flowers of the path's most notable plant, skunk cabbage. Even in one of the season's frequent rain storms it is a sight worth seeing.

The access road to the trailhead passes several large Sitka spruce, whose grayish bark and thick trunks lend them the appearance of giant columns fashioned of dark, aged concrete. More spruce surround the parking area at the trailhead. From there the hiking route proceeds west, crossing an alder-shaded creek canyon on an earthen bridge and then following an old logging road along the hillside. Red alder fills many of the damp openings along the trail's early stages and can be seen across the canyon at 0.35 mile, covering an old cutblock that was logged in the 1970s. The resultant clearcut continues over the ridge to the north, where it is visible from Highway 101. The exposed devastation shocked many passing motorists and added fuel to the drive to expand Redwood National Park. At 0.65 mile is a right-hand view down into Skunk Cabbage Creek, where a large bog is filled with the stream's namesake plant.

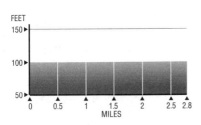

Skunk cabbage (*Lysichitum*

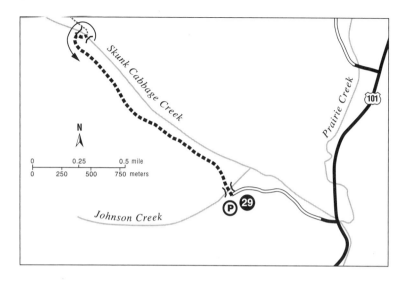

americanum) attracts attention wherever it is seen, but under the ideal growing conditions found here it will stop hikers in their tracks. Rising from a rosette of large, fleshy green leaves (some more than a yard long) is a yellow-green spadix (the plant's flower-filled spike), behind which a rich yellow bract, called a spathe, rises like a protective hood. Another name for the plant is swamp lantern, and that is the effect created by the luminous spathes as they shine brightly in the shadowed forest. Here, thousands of plants choke the stream canyon, creating a glowing flow of light like some incandescent river, tempting viewers to approach them even at the cost of traversing the muddy bogs where the plant makes its home. When flowering, skunk cabbage produces a memorable odor, intended to attract particular pollinators, that indeed justifies its name. The leaves, however, carry no such aroma and were used by certain Indian tribes for lining berry baskets and for wrapping berries and bulbs for steaming.

The forest here features both Sitka spruce and western hemlock, with a ground cover of sword fern. The trail continues to run above the boggy creek on the right, passing several large redwoods on the left at 0.95 mile. False lily-of-the-valley then appears by the trailside, as does piggy-back plant below a bridge at 1.2 miles. Soon the path turns right, moving into the broad canyon bottom before crossing Skunk Cabbage Creek at 1.4 miles. At the bridge here the route turns back to return to the trailhead.

For a longer hike: Continue past the bridge, heading west and

Along the Skunk Cabbage Creek trail

running up the rest of the canyon to the bluff top above the ocean. Turning back here adds 2.6 miles to the hike, for a total of 5.4 miles. At the bluff top you can also keep going on the Coastal Trail, first along the bluff itself and then dropping to the shoreline before reaching Gold Bluffs Beach Road. If you haven't arranged for a car shuttle here, you will need to retrace the entire route, giving your trip a total length of 11.2 miles.

30. TRILLIUM FALLS LOOP

Features	▪	a hillside redwood forest, a small waterfall, and an elk-viewing station astride Prairie Creek
Distance	▪	3.15 miles, loop
Elevation gain	▪	300 feet
Difficulty	▪	moderate
Open	▪	all year

Driving Directions: Take Highway 101 to Davison Road, 2.8 miles north of downtown Orick. Turn west on Davison Road and travel 0.3 mile to the access road for the Elk Meadow Day Use Area. Turn left on the access road and follow it 0.2 mile to a large parking area. The trailhead is at the southern end of the lot.

One of the newer trails in the park, this route is more notable for its noble redwoods and proximity to the Prairie Creek elk herd than for its small waterfall and scattering of trilliums. A springtime visit, with all four features present, is perhaps the best time for this hike, but it offers enjoyment—only a half mile from Highway 101—year-round.

Davison Road was named for early day rancher Arthur Davison and his family, whose place lay just to the north. The Davisons home-steaded there in 1889 and began a dairy operation. Soon they also opened a stopping place for travelers who came along the nearby Arcata to Crescent City wagon road. In 1902 Davison Road was built; a fifteen-man crew did the work with picks, shovels, and a horse-drawn grader called a Fresno scraper. The road climbs over a low ridge and then drops to reach the Gold Bluffs.

Your route begins at a paved walkway at the southern end of the parking lot. Soon you meet another walkway that connects with the eastern side of the lot. Turn right and proceed 50 feet to a junction with the Davison Trail. Turn right again, passing a wetland area to the

left next to Prairie Creek. In 100 yards take a dirt path to the right, the start of the Trillium Falls Trail. Ascending the hill, you enter forest, climb on switch-backs, and then follow a contour south. At 0.6 mile a steel bridge offers a right-hand view of rock-filled Trillium Falls. You then hike up another section of the slope, partly on switchbacks, before coming to a flattish benchland at the John B. DeWitt Grove at 1.15 miles. DeWitt was secretary of the Save-the-Redwoods League for many

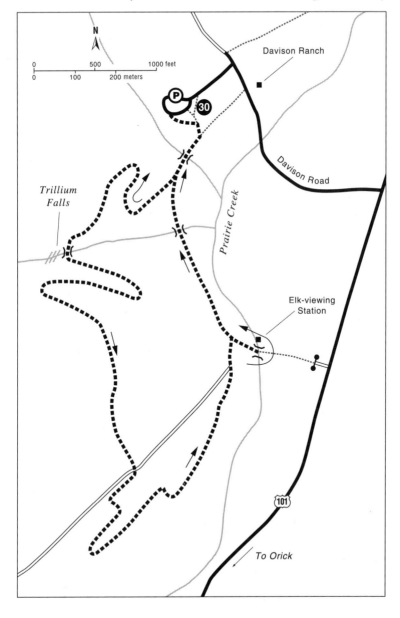

years. Look now for Pacific rhododendron and western trillium.

Western trillium (*Trillium ovatum*) is one of the preeminent wildflowers of the North Coast. The first part of its name describes its structure: tri = three, for it has three large, pointed, soft-green leaves; three petals that are brilliantly white when young but shade to pink and purple as they age; and three sepals that alternate with the petals in a sort of rosette some distance above the leaves. Also found in the park is the giant, or sessile, trillium *(Trillium chloropetalum)*, which has red or, occasionally, yellow flowers that grow upright directly from the leaves (see Hike 25).

The trail drops off the benchland, crossing a gravel road at 1.4 miles. You continue downhill amid magnificent redwoods, turning left at a large log at 1.8 miles, and then, with another left turn, heading north. Here some very big burned snags stand starkly and darkly, like exclamation points on this page of the forest.

After switchbacking downhill, you move through riparian woodland that includes salmonberry, California hazel, bigleaf maple, and red alder. At 2.5 miles the trail meets the road you crossed earlier; turn right and follow it downhill to a junction with the Davison Trail. Here you commence a short side trip by turning right, following the trail until you reach the middle of the Prairie Creek bridge. A viewing platform has been built onto the left-hand side of the bridge; it guarantees good views of the creek below and offers the possibility of seeing the

Western trillium

local elk herd. You now reverse course, turning right when you again meet the gravel road, following it back to the parking lot at 3.15 miles.

31. LOST MAN CREEK

Features ▪	stately redwoods, a pair of bridges, and an alder-shaded creek
Distance ▪	0.8 mile round trip (longer option available)
Elevation gain ▪	50 feet
Difficulty ▪	easy
Open ▪	all year

Driving Directions: Take Highway 101 to Lost Man Creek Road, 3.5 miles north of downtown Orick. Turn east and follow this gravel road 0.8 mile to the trailhead.

Warning: The two unrailed bridges on the route pose a risk for unsupervised children. Another danger is the occasional mountain biker who may come hurtling down from Holter Ridge on this multi-use trail.

No one—male or otherwise—is in danger of getting lost on this well-marked route through tall redwoods and beside an alder-shaded creek. But when an early-day timber cruiser hiked into the drainage with a partner, the partner returned but the timber cruiser didn't. Ever after the creek's name has commemorated the event. Much of the timber in the upper basin was also lost—to logging—but the lower section of the creek has retained its redwoods and lovely riparian vegetation, which form the backdrop for this scenic stroll.

The hike begins at a gate across the old logging road that rises eastward to Holter Ridge. The trail bed is gravel, and the way is wide. Large redwoods shade the roadway, while coast red elderberry, vine maple, and thimbleberry provide shrubbery to the sides. A marker at 0.1 mile notes the location where, in 1982, Redwood National Park was dedicated as a UNESCO World Heritage Site. Piggyback plant lines the way at 0.2 mile as the creek appears downslope to the right. At 0.3 mile a stout bridge spans the creek. Beyond the crossing the verdant bank to the right features lady, five-finger, sword, and deer ferns. The road bends left and crosses the

FEET
200 ▶
150 ▶
100 ▶
50 ▶
0
MILES 0.8

creek on a second bridge. Douglas's iris and Bolander's phacelia add color at the far end of the bridge. Your route turns back at 0.4 mile to regain the trailhead.

Route past picnic area

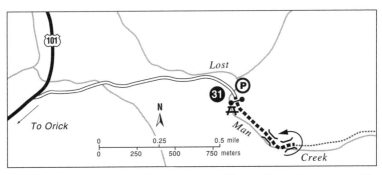

For a longer hike: Those wanting additional exertion can ramble another 0.6 mile up a less-scenic but still interesting section of the stream canyon. Beyond this point the road begins to climb steeply, soon reaching an unattractive zone of second-growth redwoods.

32. WAGON ROAD SOUTH

Features	■	a short stretch of historic roadway, some statuesque redwoods, and a glimpse of Elk Prairie
Distance	■	0.6 mile round trip
Elevation gain	■	negligible
Difficulty	■	easy
Open	■	all year

Driving Directions: Drive to mile 0.2 (9.1) of the Newton B. Drury Scenic Parkway. Turn west onto an unmarked park road. Take this gravel road 100 yards to an intersection; turn left and park in the short loop that circles back to the access road.

Want to step back a century into the past? You can walk away the decades by following this short section of the old Arcata to Crescent City wagon road to the edge of Elk Prairie.

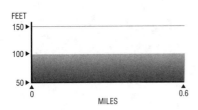

From your parking place, return to the access road, cross it, and arrive at a gate that blocks a dirt road. Proceed around the gate and head north.

In 1894 Humboldt and Del Norte Counties completed a wagon

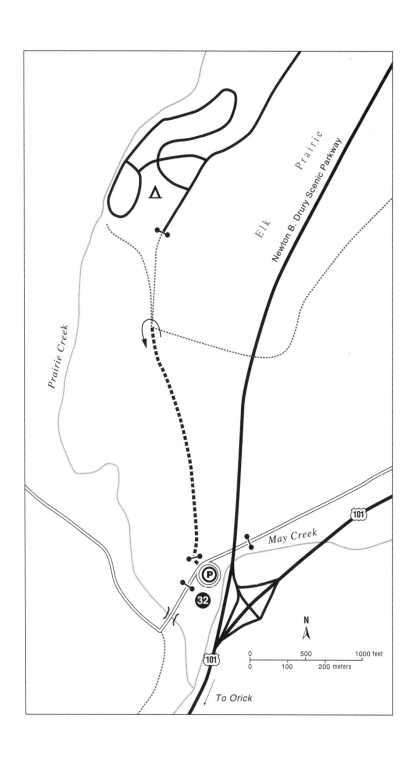

Prairie

Elk

Newton B. Drury Scenic Parkway

Prairie Creek

May Creek

101

P

32

101

N

0   500   1000 feet
0   100   200 meters

To Orick

Old county wagon road

road that linked the communities of Crescent City, to the north, and Arcata, to the south. Before then, travel between the two towns was either along a perilous combination of trails and beaches, or, perhaps equally dangerous, by ship or Indian dugout canoe. After some thirty years the wagon road was replaced by the Redwood Highway and fell into disuse, but several segments of the original route that run through the parks can still be traveled, including this picturesque section that leads from shadowy redwood forest into the sunny opening of Elk Prairie.

The duff-covered roadbed passes through medium-sized redwoods, its single lane conjuring up images of horse-drawn wagons and mud-spattered Model T's. A hundred years ago weary travelers from the south would perk up with anticipation, for just ahead lay William Boyes's farm and hotel, the latter known as Elk Tavern. Evergreen huckleberry, salmonberry, and California hazel line the road. At 0.1 mile a boggy stream is filled with skunk cabbage, while bigleaf maples extend their bright green foliage overhead. At 0.3 mile the road, which serves as part of the Davison Trail, comes out into the grassy expanse known as Elk Prairie. Your route reverses course here at the junction with the Elk Prairie Trail (see Hike 45), finishing at 0.6 mile.

For a longer hike: You can continue along the edge of the prairie in either direction on the Elk Prairie Trail; to the left are the Elk Prairie Campground and Visitor Center, to the right are the Parkway and a stand of magnificent hillside redwoods. All four features are available if you choose to complete the entire Elk Prairie Loop, which adds 2.6 miles to the hike.

PRAIRIE CREEK TO DEL NORTE COAST

33. MARSHALL POND

Features	▪	a historic bridge remnant, a beaver and otter pond, and a hillside of old-growth redwoods
Distance	▪	2.0 miles round trip (longer option available)
Elevation gain	▪	200 feet
Difficulty	▪	moderate
Open	▪	all year

Driving directions: Take Highway 101 to Klamath Beach Road, 0.5 mile south of the Klamath River. Take Klamath Beach Road 1.4 miles west to a junction with Alder Camp Road on the left. Turn onto Alder Camp Road and immediately turn right into the parking area.

Want to see a beaver dam? An otter slide? If these twin treats aren't enough for you, how about a waterfowl-filled pond and a haunting hillside redwood forest? You'll find them all on this enchanting but nearly hidden trail just a few minutes from Highway 101.

Before starting the hike, you may want to cross Klamath Beach Road and walk on a short section of the old Douglas Memorial Bridge, which is still adorned with a pair of large concrete bears at its entrance. When the bridge opened in 1926 it formed the last link in the Redwood Highway that ran from Sausalito, just north of San Francisco Bay, to Grants·Pass, Oregon. It replaced a ferry that had itself replaced a Yurok Indian paddling a redwood canoe. The bridge lasted thirty-eight years—

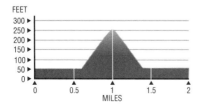

until the epic 1964 flood washed most of it away, leaving this south-shore remnant to remind us of the power of nature. Before leaving the bridge, you might want to reach up and pet one of the concrete bears—after all, they have been guarding the bridge for three quarters of a century and deserve a few strokes.

Once back at the parking lot, walk about 100 feet south to the trailhead, which is next to a sign on the right that reads, "Coastal Trail: Flint Ridge Section." The shaded path drops through a red alder thicket, making a pair of left turns that lead you to Marshall Pond, created in the 1940s to hold logs for the lumber mill that occupied the clearing to the right. The path meets the pond at 0.1 mile. Look down to the left and you should see a carefully arranged construction of small tree trunks that traps the water in the pond—a beaver dam! If you are very patient and very quiet, you might notice a V-shaped ripple followed by a row of bubbles rising through the water. If you wait even longer, you might see a pair of brown humps emerge from the pond— the head and back of one of the resident beaver engineers, bringing another stick to just the right place in the dam.

The trail turns right near the dam overlook. Watch for an opening in the vegetation on your left where it appears that something has been slithering in the mud. And something has—this is a slide that river otters, playful critters that they are, use to splash into the water. You can see another slide past the beaver dam on the far side of the pond.

Your route now follows the edge of the pond. You bend right, leave the waterside, turn left at two junctions, cross through a small open area, and regain the shore of the pond at 0.45 mile. In times past the beavers have occasionally felled an alder here; look for pointed stumps with gnaw marks on them made by the beavers' strong and useful teeth. Out on the water are great blue herons, cormorants,

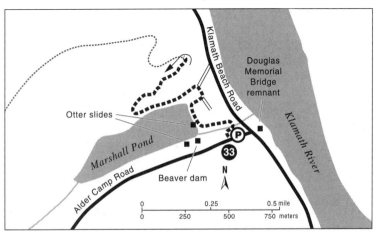

Bear at end of Douglas Memorial Bridge

and various ducks, along with lots of yellow pond-lilies. Zooming above the pond and through the trees is the occasional kingfisher, who will abruptly rasp out a chattering call that sounds like a wildly spinning ratchet wrench.

At 0.55 mile the trail begins climbing on an old roadbed, switchbacks to the right, and continues rising through a lovely old-growth forest. You have exchanged the flatness of the pond for the ranks of great verticals—the dark trunks of centuries-old redwoods rise from the surrounding ferns and bushes until they are lost in an inky green fog of foliage far above. As delicate as the trees are massive, the cloverlike leaves of oxalis, a.k.a. redwood sorrel, carpet much of the forest floor. Although you have been on the trail for only 30 minutes, you feel like you have hiked back a thousand years in time.

Two gullies are spanned by small redwood bridges; the latter is followed by a cluster of vine maples that spreads a cloud of delicate leaves above the trail. A switchback at 0.95 mile is followed by another at 1 mile. In the vicinity are several Pacific rhododendrons; look for their large pink flowers if you are hiking here in June.

The hike reverses course here. You retrace your route to the parking lot at 2.0 miles. On the way back be sure to look closely at the pond; you are seeing it from different angles and who knows what water-loving wildlife might be visible.

For a longer hike: Continue on the Flint Ridge Trail, climbing high on the ridge side through a continuation of the redwood forest. The route eventually switchbacks downhill and then crosses through an alder grove. At 3.8 miles the path cuts through a gap in Flint Ridge, reaches a crest, and then drops toward the ocean. A spur trail to the right at 4.65 miles leads to the Flint Ridge Primitive Camp. The main route continues downhill through the site of the old Hamilton-Chapman-Crivelli Ranch. In addition to raising cattle, one-time owner Ed Chapman was known to keep a pet buffalo. The trail ends at 4.8 miles, where it meets a gravel road called Coastal Drive. At the parking lot across the road a pathway drops toward the blue Pacific. You can either arrange a car shuttle here (via Klamath Beach Road and Coastal Drive) or return along the Flint Ridge route, which will give you a 9.4-mile round-trip hike.

34. MOUTH OF KLAMATH OVERLOOK

Features	▪	terrific views of the Klamath River and nearby coastline
Distance	▪	1.1 miles
Elevation gain	▪	350 feet
Difficulty	▪	strenuous
Open	▪	all year

Driving directions: Take Highway 101 to Requa Road, 3.2 miles north of the Klamath River bridge. Turn west on Requa Road, following it through the tiny town of Requa, where the road's name changes to Patrick J. Murphy Memorial Drive, and continue to the parking area for the Klamath Overlook, 2.3 miles from the junction with Highway 101.

The Klamath River drains much of northwestern California in addition to a bit of southern Oregon. Its exit into the Pacific Ocean is dramatic, and there is no better place to view it than from the over-

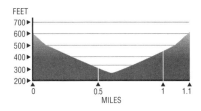

look reached by this hike.

The route starts on the Hidden Beach Section, Coastal Trail at the southern end of the trailhead parking area. The view from the lot is spectacular, but it will soon improve. A narrow, steep, and sometimes rocky trailbed mandates caution during the descent. Blackberry and coyote brush are prominent, while an absence of large trees aids observation of the ocean. At 0.1 mile is a junction. The Coastal Trail continues to the right, while the hiking route turns left, promptly cresting a small ridgeline and providing a preliminary view of the mouth of the Klamath.

Switchbacks alternate with curving sections of the trail that cling to the steep hillside. Watch for ospreys near the river mouth below. A narrow section of pathway at 0.4 mile crosses the face of a rocky cliff and calls for close attention. A series of steps then takes you downward at a faster rate, and switchbacks bring you to a stand of thimbleberry. A

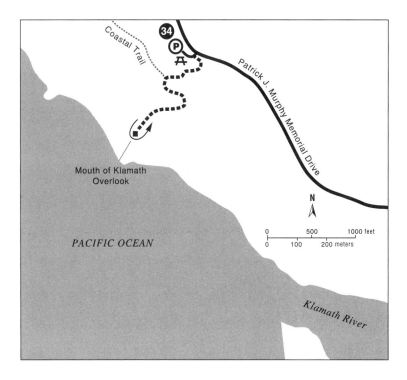

railed walkway then leads across a short saddle and up to the overlook, which perches above the splashing Pacific.

The view north is of the rocky coastline and the steep cliffs that lead to it. To the west is the cerulean sea, stretching away beyond sight. Southward, another section of the coast continues into Humboldt County, while to the southeast lies the most dramatic sight of all, that of the Klamath River issuing out of its wide canyon into the ocean. A broad sandspit stretches across most of the opening, shifting occasionally to accommodate the repositioning of the river mouth. In the distance the old Crescent City to Arcata wagon road, now part of the park's Coastal Drive, is etched on the hillside, descending to the far riverbank where the Klamath ferry once crossed. Close at hand is a massive rock column known to the Yurok Indians as Oregos. According to one tradition, Oregos is a woman who sits at the northern bank of the Klamath; when she shifts her legs the river mouth moves from north to south or vice versa. The craggy coastline north of Oregos was the site, in 1914, of the wreck of the schooner *Katata*, which had just left Requa with a load of salmon from the town's cannery. The boat was a total loss, but many cases of its cargo washed safely ashore as the canned salmon made an unexpected last migration from the sea.

After sampling the manifest sights from the overlook, it is time to retrace the route, which now becomes a pulse-rate-raising climb, reaching the parking lot at 1.1 miles.

35. HIDDEN BEACH

Features ▪	bluff-top views of the Pacific, many wildflowers, and a beautiful driftwood-rimmed beach
Distance ▪	6.2 miles round trip
Elevation gain ▪	500 feet
Difficulty ▪	strenuous
Open ▪	all year

Driving directions: Take Highway 101 to Requa Road, 3.2 miles north of the Klamath River bridge. Turn west on Requa Road, following it through the small community of Requa, where the road's name changes to Patrick J. Murphy Memorial Drive, and

Opposite: *Mouth of the Klamath River, Flint Ridge in background*

continue to the parking area for the Klamath Overlook, 2.3 miles from the junction with Highway 101.

For wide-ranging views of the ocean, this section of the Coastal Trail is tough to beat. Hidden Beach, at the route's end, makes a charming picnic spot.

The trail leaves the southern end of the parking lot by dropping quickly on a narrow and rocky path. The view to the left is of the Klamath River's meeting with the sea. A side trail to the left at 0.1

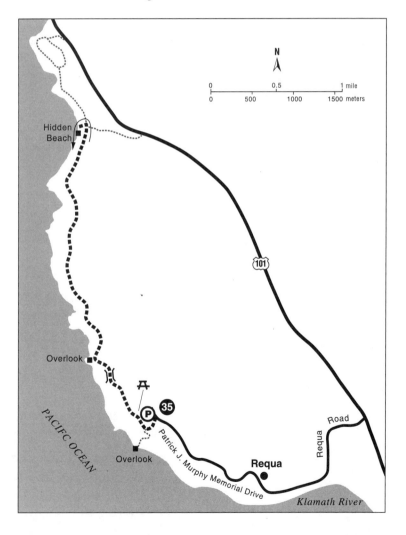

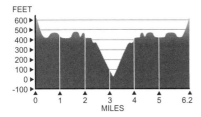

mile leads to the Klamath Overlook (see Hike 34). Bearing to the right the route continues to drop, moving across the steep hillside while passing cascara, blue coast lupine, firecracker flower, and cow parsnip. A stream canyon at 0.4 mile is shaded by Sitka spruce and red alder and fringed with thimbleberry. The trail then rises to reach an overlook at 0.6 mile that looks down upon a wide sweep of ocean and a rocky point to the north.

Now the route runs through a corridor of bushes, soon reaching a thicket of red alder. An old roadbed follows the probable remnant of a track cut by early-day rancher Louis DeMartin from his place on Wilson Creek, several miles north, to Requa.

A side trail to the right at 1.0 mile leads a few feet to an alder-shaded pond. The main route passes Douglas's iris, crimson columbine, and various violets, entering an open area that offers a view of the ocean. The path then moves into forest, dropping past numerous

Hidden Beach looking south

ferns before again picking up the old roadbed. Soon the route climbs; much of the way here is through red alder. Watch for a vista of distant Crescent City to the left. Another view, this one featuring False Klamath Rock, appears at 2.1 miles. Coast red elderberry, thimbleberry, and salmonberry line the path. The trail begins a gradual descent, leveling before meeting a right-hand trail at 3.0 miles that leads to Highway 101 at the Trees of Mystery. Continuing to the left, the hiking route promptly reaches a left-hand spur trail, which it follows 50 yards downhill to Hidden Beach.

A band of driftwood lines the upper edge of the beach. Be careful not to slip when walking over the jumbled wood. The beach itself sweeps both north and south in a gentle arc, terminating at its southern end near a craggy offshore rock. The crescent-shaped shore nestles beneath a low bluff, creating a feeling of privacy and protective enclosure.

From the beach, the route reverses direction, returning to the trailhead at 6.2 miles.

For a longer hike: Continue on the Coastal Trail past the Hidden Beach turnoff, connecting with the Yurok Loop (Hike 36) before reaching the Lagoon Creek Picnic Area, where you reverse course. This extension adds 2 miles to the hike, unless arrangements have been made for a car shuttle at the picnic area.

36. YUROK LOOP

Features	▪	spectacular views of the seacoast, proximity to a Yurok village site, and a pond full of— what else?—pond-lilies
Distance	▪	1.15 miles, loop (longer options available)
Elevation gain	▪	50 feet
Difficulty	▪	easy
Open	▪	year round

Driving directions: Take Highway 101 to the Lagoon Creek Picnic Area, 6.9 miles north of the Klamath River bridge.

No other trail in the parks offers such dramatic coastal scenery so close to the highway. A pondside picnic area makes this an ideal stop for a short, appetite-inducing hike and then . . . lunch.

The Lagoon Creek Picnic Area is adjacent to a placid, picturesque pond. In times past, the pond was a lake, known to the Yuroks as

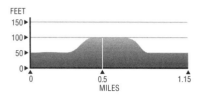

O-kwego O-keto. The lake, which was fed by the stream now called Lagoon Creek, continued towards the ocean, ending in a lagoon at the beach. The Yurok village of O'men was situated nearby. During World War II a plywood mill was built where the picnic area is now located and the lake was converted into a millpond. The mill operators fouled the water with toxic chemicals, but the problem went undetected for over half a century. Now, because of the recently discovered pollution, the pond is off limits for fishing, but a partial covering of yellow pond-lily is apparently unaffected by the contamination.

Yellow pond-lily (*Nuphar polyspalum*), also called spatterdock, is found in shallow freshwater areas. It produces thick, elongated heart-shaped leaves that may measure up to a foot and a half across. From May to October it will also display a cup-shaped, lemon-yellow flower that rises on its own stem above the leaves. The flower smells like brandy, thereby attracting pollinating insects. Its seeds were eaten by northwestern Indians, and its roots used medicinally. In recent times yellow pond-lily has been used as an aquarium and garden plant—a tribute to both its hardiness and attractiveness.

The path begins at the northern end of the parking lot, where it plunges into a thicket of red alder and willow, and soon arrives at a junction with the Coastal Trail. Turn left, crossing a bridge over Lagoon Creek. The route follows an old road that once led out to and

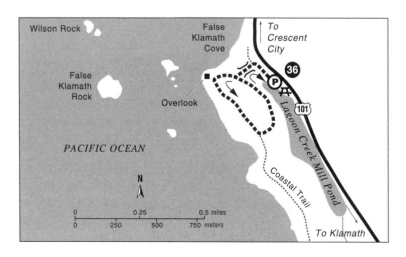

False Klamath Rock

around the point. On the right is a view of the beach at False Klamath Cove. In early days, ship captains sometimes mistook the cove for the mouth of the Klamath River, hence the name.

You reach a junction at 0.15 mile where the two ends of the loop trail meet. Go right, passing through another corridor of vegetation and reaching an open point. The view is spectacular, rivaling the best along the coast. To the south is the curving sweep of Hidden Beach, while directly west lies the large mass of False Klamath Rock, with smaller Wilson Rock to the northwest. Northeastward stretches False Klamath Cove, with Highway 101 rising in the distance over the Wilson Creek bridge. The creek was once the boundary between the Yurok and Tolowa Indian tribes. To the left of the bridge the coastline runs northwest, reaching to the dramatic domes of Footsteps Rocks before turning northward. In the far distance the flatlands at Crescent City can sometimes be discerned.

Yurok villages along the coast were located either at the mouths of creeks or rivers, or at lagoons. Other members of the tribe lived along the lower Klamath River on terraces above the reach of floodwaters. All Yuroks consumed salmon and other fish as a main part of their diet, but those living on the coast also had access to shellfish and to the marine mammals that lived on the offshore rocks. Yurok canoes, carefully crafted out of sections of old-growth redwood, were held in the highest regard, and other tribes would readily trade for them. In their canoes, the Yuroks of O'men ventured into the perilous Pacific in search of food and also to reach other villages. The offshore rocks that seem so remote to us would no doubt have been frequented by the Yuroks, since they served for the Indians as a sort of neighborhood grocery store, stocked with such delicacies as seals, sea lions, and various edible plants.

Now the route turns south, running along the side of the hill that separates the ocean from the pond. You pass cow parsnip and silk tassel, red alder and Sitka spruce. Upon reaching a junction at 0.6 mile, the Coastal Trail bears right, continuing on to Hidden Beach and the Requa area (see Hike 35). Turn left, following the loop trail around the hill past red elderberry and more alders. The pond is now to your right, obscured by thick foliage. At mile 1 you complete the loop, turn right, and retrace the initial part of your route back returning to the trailhead at 1.15 miles.

For a longer hike: You can continue south on the Coastal Trail to Hidden Beach, or, if you're especially ambitious, go all the way to the Klamath Overlook above Requa. Hike 35 describes most of this route.

37. WAGON ROAD NORTH

Features	▪	a hillside forest, a vista of the coast, and an historic road
Distance	▪	4.0 miles
Elevation gain	▪	200 feet
Difficulty	▪	moderate
Open	▪	all year

Driving directions: Take Highway 101 to Wilson Creek Road, 7.7 miles north of the Klamath River bridge. Turn right onto Wilson Creek Road and park at the pulloff immediately to your right.

Travel has never been easy along California's North Coast, but until the 1890s it was especially difficult to go overland from Humboldt Bay to Crescent City. The combination of primitive trails and beach traverses precluded the use of wagons or stages, making the often perilous alternative, passage by ship, attractive by comparison. In 1894 a "road" was completed that connected the commercial centers of Humboldt and Del Norte Counties, but it was only in 1898, after additional improvements, that it was able to accommodate wagon traffic.

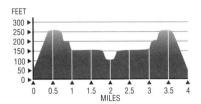

This hike travels part of the northern segment of the route, the Crescent City and Klamath River Wagon Road.

The trailhead is just past the parking pullout at the entrance to the Redwood Hostel, which perches on the hill above. Hike around a

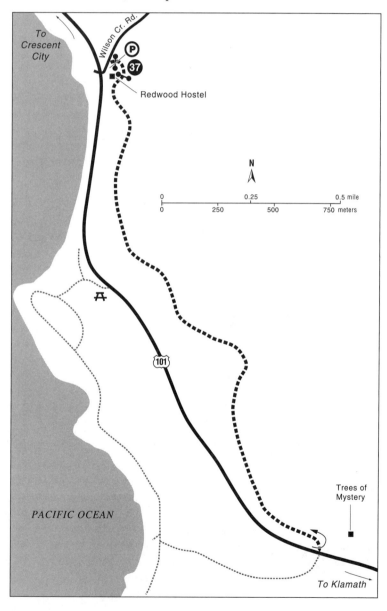

steel gate, which bars vehicular access during the daytime hours that the hostel is closed (10 A.M. to 5 P.M.), and proceed up the driveway to another gate at mile 0.1. Go around this gate also and continue uphill on a dirt roadbed, past outbuildings of the hostel.

The Redwood Hostel itself is a sturdy, shingled building, dating from about 1908, that was once the home of the DeMartin family. Agnes and Louis DeMartin settled here in 1877, established a ranch, and raised a large family. The trail to Crescent City was so bad that Louis DeMartin hired local Indians to transport his goods in dugout canoes. Periodically Agnes DeMartin would also make the canoe trip, bringing with her their latest child, who had to be taken to Crescent City for baptizing. Needless to say, Louis DeMartin was a strong advocate of the coastal wagon road, and he constructed the section that ran past his ranch, including a bridge over Wilson Creek. Some sixty years later the new highway bridge across the creek was named in his honor.

Continue uphill, trodding on DeMartin's section of the old road,

DeMartin House

passing coast red elderberry and Chilean aster, western coltsfoot and western wax myrtle. The roadbed crests on the wooded hillside at 0.4 mile, where a right-hand vista emerges of False Klamath Cove and Footsteps Rocks. From here the route begins a gentle, undulating decline that will last the rest of its course. Sitka spruce and red alder compose most of the forest, while salmonberry and thimbleberry occupy openings in the canopy. At 1.3 miles a pair of small streams host piggy-back plants in the moist soil. A short distance ahead an especially large redwood rises to the left. The route then drops more earnestly, reaching an opening at 2.0 miles. Just ahead is a large, paved parking lot, and beyond it the arresting sight of a large blue bovine and an even larger, red-shirted, bearded woodsman—Paul Bunyan and his ox, Babe. They constitute the iconic entry pieces to a tourist stop known as the Trees of Mystery.

Here the hiking route turns back, leaving the startling sights of the present to regain the 1894 wagon road, on which numerous horses of varying colors once traveled but nary, it is safe to say, a blue ox. You reach the trailhead at 4.0 miles.

For a longer hike: Bear right along the edge of the Trees of Mystery parking lot to Highway 101. Cross it, using great caution, and take the Hidden Beach Trail through the boglands of upper Lagoon Creek to Hidden Beach (see Hike 35). After leaving the beach, proceed north on the Coastal Trail, taking the western section of the Yurok Loop (see Hike 36), and then depart from it on the Coastal Trail to follow the edge of False Klamath Cove. Proceed along the western side of Highway 101 until you reach the junction with Wilson Creek Road, and then cautiously recross the highway to the parking area.

DEL NORTE COAST TO JEDEDIAH SMITH

38. NICKEL CREEK–ENDERTS BEACH

Features ■	remnants of the original Redwood Highway, an intriguing stream canyon, and a secluded beach
Distance ■	2.0 miles
Elevation gain ■	200 feet
Difficulty ■	moderate
Open ■	all year

Driving directions: Take Highway 101 to Enderts Beach Road, 2.4 miles south of Crescent City. Turn south on Enderts Beach Road and drive 2.3 miles to the parking area at the end of the road. The trailhead is at the southern end of the parking lot.

The coastline south of Crescent City has long been a formidable barrier to overland travel. The county wagon road, built in the 1890s, stayed on the beach for as far as it could and then climbed onto the slope above the ocean. It then ran briefly above Nickel Creek before switchbacking up to the redwood-filled ridgeline to the east. When the Redwood Highway came through three decades later, the design engineers conceived a bold stoke: have the roadway angle down from the ridge, crossing the steep cliffs south of Nickel Creek. This plan assured travelers of some of the most spectacular coastal views available on any thoroughfare, and it also ensured disaster. Within a few years much of the highway was slipping into the sea, and soon the road was rerouted ridgeward, where it ran close to its predecessor, the old county road.

Enderts Beach Road is itself a renovated section of the Redwood Highway. It is blocked off at the trailhead parking area, where the Last Chance Section, Coast Trail, begins. Take this route south, following the old highway, which here is cut into the cliff some 200 feet above the

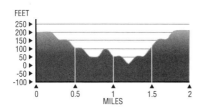

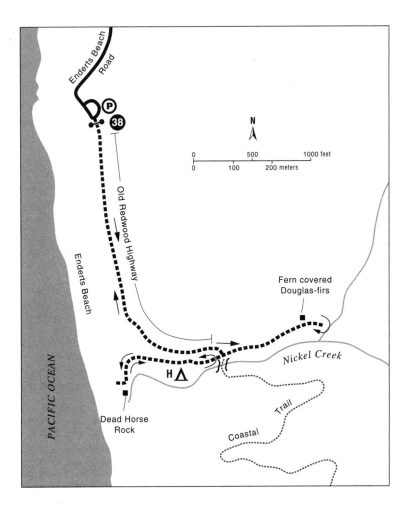

ocean. Chilean aster, coast red elderberry, coyote brush, and red alder line the roadbed. At 0.1 mile you'll see a distant view south of a sheer cliff face, its surface scratched by a broken diagonal line—all that remains of the Redwood Highway.

The trail enters a corridor of vegetation composed of red alder, conifers, coastal silk tassel, and western wax myrtle. Soon red flowering currant, cascara, fireweed, and blueblossom appear along the path. You arrive at an intersection at 0.5 mile. The Coastal Trail continues straight ahead, immediately crossing Nickel Creek and then departing from the course of the old Redwood Highway; it is a worthy route but not part of the current hike. Turn left instead, following an old roadbed up the canyon of Nickel Creek. Bigleaf maple, California hazel, and snowberry bring color here in fall. At 0.65 mile several large Douglas-firs come into view, the limbs and trunk of each clad in numerous leather ferns, as if part of some strange coniferous jungle. The route continues a short distance to a huge Sitka spruce, where the roadbed vanishes into the vegetation. A narrow path continues across a side creek, but the hiking route reverses course here, returning to the intersection at 0.9 mile. This time your way is straight ahead, continuing to follow the alder-filled canyon of Nickel Creek downstream.

A side trail to the Nickel Creek Primitive Camp branches left next to the camp's restroom. Continue to the right, rising briefly to an overlook of the ocean and then bending to the left. The trail promptly drops and runs out onto a narrow, rocky ridgelet that projects itself between Nickel Creek on the left and Enderts Beach on the right. Near the tip of the ridgelet you turn right and carefully climb down the rocks to Enderts Beach, at 1.2 miles. To the left, just around the tip of the point, is the mouth of Nickel Creek. Notice a large hole in the rock mass that forms the point. Long ago, a mail carrier named Smith, while heading south towards Requa, lost his mail horse in the creek. The animal was carried down to the beach, where it tried to escape by going through

Along old Highway 101 near Enderts Beach

the hole in the rock, where it became stuck and drowned. Ever after, the mail rider was known as "Dead Horse" Smith.

You may want to hike either north or south along Enderts Beach (keeping a careful eye on the tide and remembering what happened to "Dead Horse" Smith's namesake) before reversing course to return first to the intersection at 1.5 miles, and then, turning left, to the trailhead at 2.0 miles.

For a longer hike: At the intersection, continue south on the Coastal Trail, crossing Nickel Creek and then immediately turning left at a junction, leaving the old highway as you climb the south side of the creek canyon. Eventually this trail will connect you with Old Highway 101 North (Hike 56), which you can take to that hike's trailhead if you've arranged a car shuttle.

39. CRESCENT BEACH OVERLOOK

Features ▪	wetlands, woodlands, and a climb to a promontory that overlooks a pair of crescents—city and beach
Distance ▪	4.0 miles round trip
Elevation gain ▪	200 feet
Difficulty ▪	moderate
Open ▪	all year

Driving directions: Take Highway 101 to Enderts Beach Road, 2.4 miles south of Crescent City. Turn south on Enderts Beach Road and drive 0.6 mile to the access road for the Crescent Beach Picnic Area. Turn right and follow the access road 0.2 mile to a parking lot.

The wide sweep of sea that runs from Crescent City southward splashes against a stunning section of the northern California coastline, and it is best seen from the overlook at the end of this engaging trail.

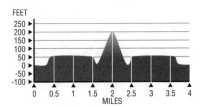

The hike leaves the parking lot by doubling back on the access road 0.1 mile to the start of the Crescent Beach Coastal Trail which is located to your right. Here you turn onto a grassy track whose irregular surface is also

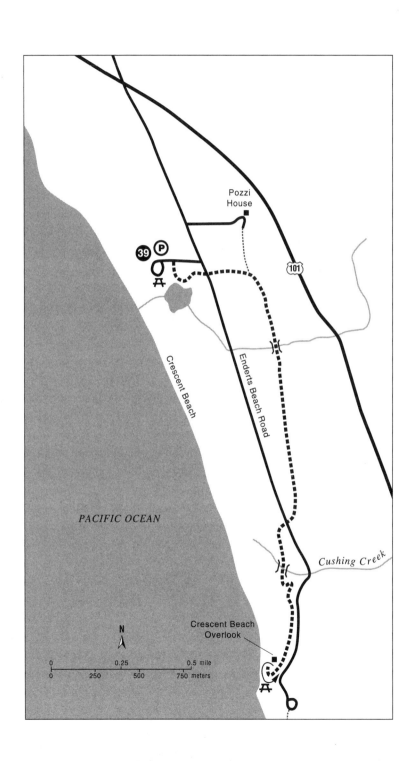

Pozzi
House

39 Ⓟ

101

Crescent Beach

Enderts Beach Road

PACIFIC OCEAN

Cushing Creek

Crescent Beach
Overlook

N

| 0 | 0.25 | 0.5 mile |
| 0 | 250 | 500 | 750 meters |

pocked with gopher and mole holes. Queen Anne's lace, coyote brush, and Douglas's iris grow at the pathside. The trail bends to go under and around a Sitka spruce, passes a sedge-filled wetland on the right and then crosses Enderts Beach Road at 0.2 mile. Hike through a grassy meadow, presently arriving at a junction where you turn right. The way left leads to a park residence, called the Pozzi House, which was once the headquarters of Alexander/Pozzi Ranch. Henry Alexander started the operation in 1869 and ran sheep, cattle, and dairy cows, the latter of which produced two tons of butter in 1879. The Pozzi family bought the ranch in 1914 and operated it until the park purchased the property in the 1980s.

There is no livestock to be observed here now, so instead look and listen for various shrub-loving birds. After passing through an open area, the trail enters a stand of tall, thin red alder, beneath which is an understory of coast red elderberry. The route crosses a bridge at 0.65 mile and enters a corridor of cascara. The numerous leafy, round trees have an orderliness that makes them seem part of an orchard.

Cascara (*Rhamnus purshiana*) almost perished as a species because of its usefulness. For years the bark of this small tree served as the country's most popular commercial laxative, but overharvesting led to near extinction before a decline in the cathartic market granted cascara a reprieve. Economic value aside, the plant is worthy of attention for its thin, dark gray trunk, which sometimes twists into striking contortions, and, in fall, for the delicate coloring of its leaves, which often add an orange tinting as they change from green to yellow. In coastal areas, where autumnal hues are often subdued, cascara makes an appropriate addition.

The trail continues southward, passing over a series of bridges and encountering more red alder and cascara before recrossing Enderts Beach Road at 1.4 miles. After cutting through a grassy opening, the path drops into the spruce- and alder-shaded gulch of Cushing Creek, which is spanned by an S-shaped bridge. Steps, a switchback, and more steps take the trail uphill, until it reaches Enderts Beach Road at 1.85 miles. Now the route runs briefly beside the road, still climbing, before veering off and cresting a hump on the hillside known as White Knob. The trail then follows a paved walkway, bearing right at a junction to reach the Crescent Beach Overlook. The view north from here is stunning: the beach below is a tawny, gently curving sweep of sand,

Opposite: *Crescent Beach*

extending northwestward to the waterfront of Crescent City. To the west of town the coastline crumples into the craggy mass of Battery Point, while a nearby series of offshore rocks protrudes from the ocean, having long provided peril for mariners trying to navigate into the harbor. Even the most steadfast landlubbers will feel their pulses rise as they behold this dramatic meeting of coast and sea.

From here you retrace your route to the Crescent Beach parking area at 4.0 miles.

For a longer hike: You can continue south from the overlook, following Enderts Beach Road 100 yards to its end. There you can take Hike 38, which leads to both Nickel Creek and Enderts Beach. This extension adds 1.6 miles to your trip.

PRAIRIE CREEK REDWOODS STATE PARK

The most diverse of the northernmost redwood parks, Prairie Creek offers gigantic redwoods, charming creek canyons, scenic beaches and bluffs, and several elk herds. Many of its hiking trails interconnect, allowing for numerous loop options and opportunities for seeing different combinations of habitat. For redwood-seekers on a tight schedule, Prairie Creek is thus the one "must see" park north of Eureka.

There are two sections to the park:

1) The redwood-rich canyon of Prairie Creek itself is accessible from the Newton B. Drury Scenic Parkway, a paved, two-lane road that was part of Highway 101 until a section of freeway nicknamed the Park Bypass was completed in 1992. The southern interchange for the Parkway is located on Highway 101, 5 miles north of the town of Orick; the northern interchange is on Highway 101, 4 miles south of the Klamath River. Most of the Parkway follows the park's namesake, Prairie Creek. Near the southern end is Elk Prairie, a large grassy opening in the forest. On the west side of the prairie are the park's visitor center and campground, reached by a paved access road that leaves the Parkway 1.1 miles from its southern end and 8.2 miles from its northern end. The Elk Prairie Visitor Center is located just north of the access road, a hundred yards from the parkway. It includes a well-stocked bookstore and a small natural and human history museum. Free parking is available in two small lots near the building. Several hikes start at the trailhead just to the north of the visitor center. Others start at trailheads along the Parkway. Hike descriptions located in this section of the park provide trailhead locations based on their distances from the southern end of the Parkway. (The distances from the northern end are given in parentheses.)

2) The Gold Bluffs and their adjacent beach are reached by one-lane, gravel Davison Road, which leaves Highway 101 some 2.8 miles north of downtown Orick. The narrow, curvy road is restricted to vehicles less than 8 feet wide and 24 feet long. Davison Road winds through forest and over ridges for 3.7 miles before arriving at the Gold Bluffs Entrance Station, where park day-use and camping fees are assessed. Here the road turns into Gold Bluffs Beach Road,

Roosevelt elk near Gold Bluffs

continuing another 3.2 miles before ending at a picnic area and trailhead. It provides access to a long stretch of beaches, dunes, and bluffs. Elk herds roam through much of the area. Hiking routes here either run along the bluffs or cut inland to connect with the Prairie Creek area. The Gold Bluffs Beach Campground and a second picnic area are located along the road.

Prairie Creek Redwoods State Park was established in 1923, when Zipporah Russ, widow of Humboldt County's largest landowner, donated 160 acres astride Prairie Creek to the state. It was in 1931, however, that the park really began to take shape, when the Save-the-Redwoods League acquired some 5000 acres from a timber-holding company. During the Great Depression a Civilian Conservation Corps (CCC) camp was established on Elk Prairie, and its workers developed much of the infrastructure for the park, including the construction of the charming wood-shingle building that is now the Elk Prairie Visitor Center. During this same period the park served as a "no-hunting" area that kept safe the state's last remaining herd of Roosevelt elk. In 1948 the endangered animals received further protection when the League purchased about 1800 acres of additional land, including Elk Prairie. Another noteworthy acquisition was that of Fern Canyon, whose 30 acres of vegetation-rich creek gorge became part of the park in 1965. At present, Prairie Creek offers about 75 miles of hiking trails that run mostly through old-growth redwoods and either along shaded ridge tops or through one of several stream canyons.

The park can be visited year round, but it is especially appealing in summer, when its proximity to the coast generally provides cool temperatures, and in fall, when the creekside maples color yellow and orange, brightening the enshadowed redwood forest. The campgrounds and more popular trails can be very busy during tourist season, but solitude-seekers can travel far from the madding crowds on several of our routes, especially hikes 41, 47, 48, 50, 51, and 53. *Note: driving to the trailheads for hikes 40-46 requires payment of a day-use fee.*

For a list of park facilities, see the appendix at the end of the book.

40. FERN CANYON LOOP

Features	▪	a fern-filled gorge, a historic prairie, and a unique bridge
Distance	▪	1.8 miles, loop (longer hike option available)
Elevation gain	▪	200 feet
Difficulty	▪	moderate
Open	▪	spring through fall (the plank bridges in Fern Canyon are removed in winter—check at the Gold Bluffs Entrance Station or the Elk Prairie Visitor Center for current status)

Driving directions: Take Highway 101 to Davison Road, 2.8 miles north of Orick. Turn west on Davison Road, passing the Gold Bluffs Entrance Station at 3.7 miles, where the road's name changes to Gold Bluffs Beach Road, and continue to the parking area at the road's end at 6.9 miles. The trailhead is at the northeast edge of the parking lot. *Note: to drive to the trailhead you must pay a day-use fee.*

A twisting, shadowed corridor whose walls are a green tapestry 150 feet high—no wonder Fern Canyon is one of the most widely sought locations in all the redwood parks. There is history here, too, for the bluff top above the canyon was the site of an early-day gold-mining operation.

The trail cuts its way through red alder to a junction at 0.2 mile. To the left is the Coastal Trail (see Hike 41). Go right, entering the floodplain of Home Creek. In 100 feet bear left at another junction onto the James Irvine Trail, thereby avoiding Fern Canyon for the time being and instead climbing up the bluff. Beware of stinging nettle at

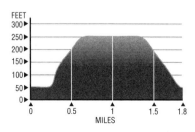

0.3 mile. Soon you cross a boggy area on a boardwalk and the trail levels. A side path to the right leads down to Alexander Lincoln Prairie, where the numerous structures of the Upper Gold Bluffs Mining Company once stood. Today there is no gold to be found here, but anyone who crosses the prairie will be offered a gilt-edged view of Fern Canyon far below. *Warning: The view from Alexander Lincoln Prairie down into Fern Canyon is stunning, but approaching the edge of the bluff is dangerous. Parents should closely supervise children.*

The route continues through a stand of Sitka spruce, reaching a junction at 0.5 mile. To the right is Fern Canyon. You postpone its pleasures yet again, bearing left. The Friendship Ridge Trail forks left at 0.75 mile; go right, carefully avoiding the many large snakelike roots that seem immobilized in mid-wriggle across the path. In 100 yards you reach a narrow chasm spanned by the John Glascock Baldwin Bridge, in the center of which are two chairs that face each other and offer upstream canyon views, including a gleaming thread of a waterfall and many ferns. Near the right side of the bridge is a redwood that has fallen across the canyon. Still alive, two of its limbs have grown skyward like small trees.

Turn around at the bridge, retracing your route until you reach the Fern Canyon Trail at 1.1 mile. Turn left onto it, dropping quickly on stairs into the canyon. Once at its base, follow Home Creek downstream, crossing it at intervals on seasonal plank bridges. Ferns—especially five-fingered—glow green all the way downcanyon, but they increase in number as you near the canyon mouth. Rounding each bend reveals a yet-more-spectacular display of greenery, as clasp-

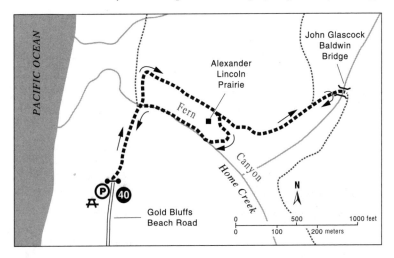

Five-finger fern, the canyon's most common plant

ing twisted stalk subtly intermixes with the other plants. On a busy day the deeply shaded canyon is illuminated innumerable times by flashbulbs that futilely try to emulate the foliage-screened sun.

At 1.55 miles you reach the canyon mouth and the junction with the James Irvine Trail. Bear left here and do likewise at the junction just ahead, returning to the trailhead at 1.8 miles.

For a longer hike: At the Baldwin Bridge, continue on the James Irvine Trail another mile, following the drainage of Home Creek upstream. Along the way you will cross two deep defiles that side streams have cut into the conglomerate rock of the canyon bed. A good turn-around point is where the trail crosses Home Creek and begins to climb out of the drainage.

41. GOLD BLUFFS–GOLD DUST FALLS

Features	∎	red alder thickets, transient elk, the Gold Bluffs, and a pair of stunning waterfalls
Distance	∎	3 miles
Elevation gain	∎	negligible
Difficulty	∎	moderate
Open	∎	all year

Driving directions: Take Highway 101 to Davison Road, 2.8 miles north of Orick. Turn west on Davison Road, passing the Gold Bluffs

Entrance Station at 3.7 miles, where the road's name changes to Gold Bluffs Beach Road. Continue to the parking area at the road's end at 6.9 miles. The trailhead is at the northeast edge of the parking lot. *Note: to drive to the trailhead you must pay a day-use fee.*

Autos used this route until the 1960s; now mountain bikes make most of the trips along it. You will be an oddity as a hiker here, but you will quickly discover the multiple attractions that others are missing.

Leaving the edge of the parking lot, the path runs northward through red alders that congregate on the slope below the bluffs, reaching a junction at 0.2 mile. Right leads to Fern Canyon (see Hike 40) and the James Irvine Trail. Go left, crossing through the spew of stones and pebbles that marks the various courses of Fern Canyon's Home Creek. The path sometimes becomes indistinct, but the keen-eyed will soon find a plank spanning Home Creek. The path continues through the rocks, reaching a thicket of young alders and then crossing Boat Creek at 0.45 mile, where a footlog may be present; otherwise, it is time to be thankful you are wearing waterproof boots.

You emerge from the rocky riparian zone to see sand dunes in the distance to the left. A wetland is closer at hand, and nearer yet (in late summer) grows a purple-gray cloud of pennyroyal. At 0.7 mile you enter a striking stand of red alder, their tall, thin, gray-white trunks waiting to sway in the slightest breeze. The route continues along the old roadbed that once ran to Ossagon Creek and then climbed, with extreme steepness, over the ridge to meet the Redwood Highway next to Prairie Creek. The trail skirts the edge of a landslide at mile 1. Looking right gives you a clear view of the culprit, a decomposing section of the Gold Bluffs that towers far above the trail. In the nineteenth century the beach was much narrower, and waves would regularly sweep all the way to the base of the bluffs, often causing sections of the tightly packed gold-bearing conglomerate to fall to the ground far below. A mining operation based on the prairie above Fern Canyon used a string of mules to carry the black sand from the freshly broken bluff back to the prairie, where the material was run through sluice boxes and a meager amount of gold extracted.

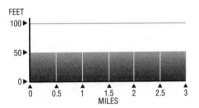

The trail follows the roadbed, staying close to the base of the bluffs. A cluster of spruce-shaded

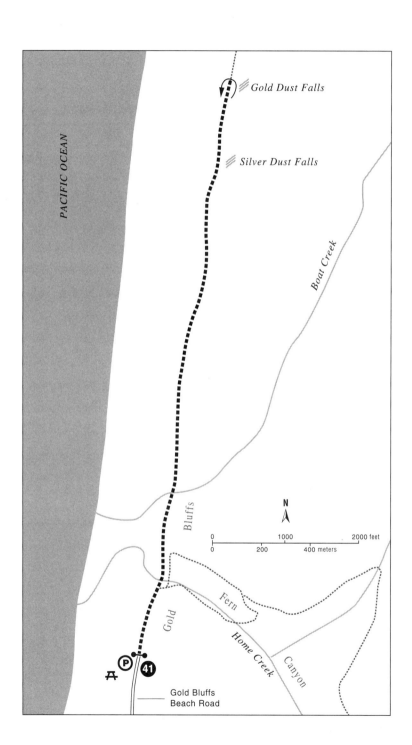

PACIFIC OCEAN

Gold Dust Falls

Silver Dust Falls

Boat Creek

Bluffs

N

| 0 | | 1000 | | 2000 feet |
| 0 | 200 | 400 meters | | |

Fern

Gold

Home Creek

Canyon

Gold Bluffs
Beach Road

41

The Gold Bluffs

sedges at 1.3 miles announces Silver Dust Falls on the right, a sparkling spill of water that cuts through the top of the bluff and then runs down the cliff. Continue to another spruce grove at 1.5 miles, where a park sign on the right signals Gold Dust Falls, which is difficult to approach due to dense vegetation. The water flow here is greater than that of its predecessor, and its spray moistens not only the pebbly bluff directly behind the falls, but also, to both sides, a dark green cladding of moss and, beyond that, a tapestry of five-finger fern.

Turn south here and head back to the trailhead. It is easy to extend the hike by making a foray into the dunes or going all the way to the beach. You may also want to pause and observe, from a safe distance, any Roosevelt elk that happen to be in the vicinity. If you stay on the trail, however, you'll reach the parking lot at 3 miles.

42. NATURE LOOP

Features ■	large streamside redwoods, a short hillside climb, and lots of fall color
Distance ■	0.9 mile loop
Elevation gain ■	100 feet
Difficulty ■	easy
Open ■	summer only when hiked as a loop (the summer bridge across Prairie Creek is taken out for the rainy season—check at the entrance station or visitor center for status); the trail can also be hiked out and back to the creek crossing, which adds 0.1 mile

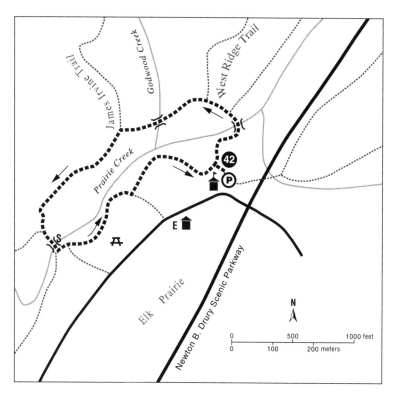

Driving directions: Drive to mile 0.4 (8.9) of the Newton B. Drury Scenic Parkway at the north end of Elk Prairie. Turn west onto the campground entrance road and go 100 yards to the Elk Prairie Visitor Center. Here you will find two parking areas (no fee), one on each side of the entrance road. After parking, walk to the northern end of the northern parking area, just past the visitor center, to reach the trailhead.

This convenient hike takes you down and back up a very pretty part of Prairie Creek, starting and finishing at the park's visitor center. Along

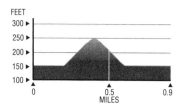

the route you'll see lots of riparian vegetation, nice views of the creek, and numerous redwoods.

Start at a paved walkway at the north end of the parking lot. In 20 feet turn right, descending past a large trailhead sign to a wooden

Prairie Creek from Nature Loop

bridge. In the gorge below flows Prairie Creek, the gravel of the creekbed visible beneath the rippling water. The trail then winds through mixed forest to a right-hand junction at 0.1 mile with the Prairie Creek Trail. Go left, soon coming close to the creek. Stay left at a junction where the West Ridge Trail departs to the right. Presently you cross Godwood Creek, where red huckleberry, California hazel, and bigleaf maple cluster. The Miner's Ridge Trail branches right at 0.2 mile, while you bear to the left.

Soon you reenter the forest, climbing steep switchbacks past California harebell and sword fern. The trail runs across the hillside, offering views of Prairie Creek to the left. Another set of s witchbacks takes you down to a junction at 0.55 mile. To the right is a continuation of the Nature Trail that currently ends downstream at the site of a year-round bridge. The bridge is awaiting replacement (check at the visitor center for current status), so turn left at the junction and drop to a summer bridge. Ascend the far bank, passing bigleaf maple, and come to a junction. Go left here and left at another junction about 100 yards ahead. Almost immediately you come to an overlook to the left that offers a lovely view of Prairie Creek. At 0.75 mile you turn left again at a junction, passing several large redwoods before arriving back at the visitor center. Cross the parking lot to reach the trailhead at 0.9 mile.

43. JAMES IRVINE–MINER'S RIDGE LOOP

Features	▪	magnificent creekside forest, a haunting hillside of redwoods, and a historic mining trail
Distance	▪	7.6 miles, loop (longer option available)
Elevation gain	▪	450 feet
Difficulty	▪	strenuous
Open	▪	all year

Driving Directions: Drive to mile 0.4 (8.9) of the Newton B. Drury Scenic Parkway at the north end of Elk Prairie. Turn west onto the campground entrance road and go 100 yards to the Elk Prairie Visitor Center. Here you will find two parking areas (no fee), one on each side of the entrance road. After parking, walk to the northern end of the northern parking area, just past the visitor center, to reach the trailhead.

Hikers on this popular route will get to sample some of the park's best canyon-bottom conifers and some striking ridge-top redwoods. A remote connecting trail offers a striking stand of remote redwoods, and near the hike's conclusion you follow the footsteps of gold miners from the nineteenth century.

Start at a paved walkway at the north end of the parking lot. In 20 feet turn right, descending past a large trailhead sign and crossing Prairie Creek on a high wooden bridge. The trail winds past large redwoods before meeting the Prairie Creek Trail at mile 0.1, which branches right. Bear left, mile 0.2, at a junction with the West Ridge Trail, following the Nature Trail across Godwood Creek to reach another junction at 0.25 mile. Here you turn right onto a rerouted section of the James Irvine Trail, climbing briefly before dropping to cross a side creek on a redwood bridge. The trail then climbs the side of Miner's Ridge, switch-backing past a display of sedimentary con-

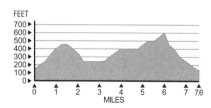

FEET
700▶
600▶
500▶
400▶
300▶
200▶
100▶
0▶
0 1 2 3 4 5 6 7 7.6
MILES

glomerate and sandstone before reaching a fork at mile 0.9. Here you bear right, continuing on the James Irvine Trail; we'll return later on the Miner's Ridge Trail, which branches left.

The trail now undulates along the side of Miner's Ridge, offering views of the lush drainage of Godwood Creek downslope to the right. At mile 1.2 the shattered stub of a fallen redwood stands at trailside, right, with eight-foot-long giant splinters nearby. The route crosses a small bridge, mile 1.55, at the far end of which is a "walk-through" redwood snag with an opening about four-and-a-half feet high. The trail begins dropping, passing under the root mass of a fallen redwood at mile 2.0. Three younger redwoods grow from the base of this "nurse log," along with several berry bushes. You continue your descent to a

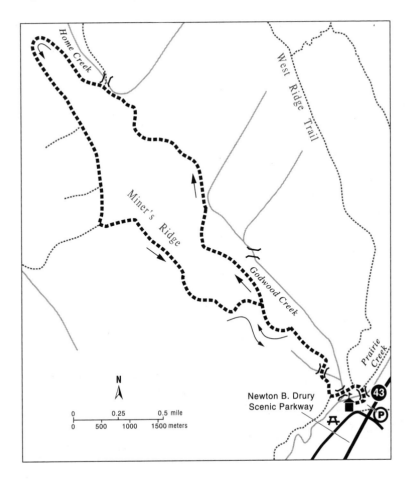

Clintonia

stream crossing, mile 2.2, climb briefly to the George J. Yamas Grove bench, and then pick up the well-worn bed of the old James Irvine Trail, which runs along the base of Miner's Ridge.

Soon you encounter a pair of fallen giants, first a spruce and then a redwood, that lie across the trail, compelling hikers to bend down to pass under them. The route returns to the canyon bottom, crosses between two sections of a large log, and approaches the base of a massive redwood at 3.2 miles. To the right a short path leads to a bench; the main trail bends left and climbs a bit of hillside. Soon it drops on steps to cross a side stream and then rises to arrive at a junction with the Clintonia Trail, mile 3.3. Turn left onto the Clintonia Trail which, however, lacks any displays of its namesake flower. They will come later, on the Miner's Ridge Trail. The route rises through a stretch of beautiful, open redwood forest, reaching the ridgeline at 3.8 miles. You pick up an old roadbed, mile 4.15, pass through partly cutover forest, and then meet the Miner's Ridge Trail at mile 4.8. Turn left, climbing eastward on the Miner's Ridge Trail, soon gaining the ridgeline. The route, which was once used by gold seekers to reach the mine above Fern Canyon, offers spectacular views down redwood-covered slopes.

At 5.8 miles you see the first of numerous clintonias that line the next stretch of path. These colorful plants first produce a cluster of cerise-colored blooms, which by midsummer are transformed into bluish purple berries. Other flowers, including fat false Solomon's seal, Columbia lily, and western trillium, soon follow. The trail begins dropping from the ridgetop at 6.05 miles, passing tiger lilies before meeting the Miner's Ridge Trail, mile 6.65. You turn right, descending to reach the Nature Trail at mile 7.35, where you turn left. Bear right at the next two trail junctions to arrive at the trailhead, mile 7.6.

For a longer hike: At the junction with the Clintonia Trail, turn right instead of left, following the James Irvine Trail down Home Creek and then dropping into Fern Canyon (see Hike 40). Hike out to the Fern Canyon trailhead and then south along Gold Bluffs Beach Road for 1.1 miles, where you meet the western end of the Miner's Ridge Trail. Take this east, turning right at its junction with the Clintonia Trail, and then follow the rest of the main hike's route for a total trip of 10.25 miles. *Note: the stretch along Gold Bluffs Beach Road is traveled frequently by cars and can be dusty in dry weather.*

44. WEST RIDGE–PRAIRIE CREEK LOOP

Features ■	a redwood-covered ridgeline, the park's namesake creek, and the wildly contorted Corkscrew Tree
Distance ■	6.45 miles, loop
Elevation gain ■	600 feet
Difficulty ■	strenuous
Open ■	all year

Driving directions: Drive to mile 0.4 (8.9) of the Newton B. Drury Scenic Parkway at the north end of Elk Prairie. Turn west onto the campground entrance road and go 100 yards to the Elk Prairie Visitor Center. Here you will find two parking areas (no fee), one on each side of the entrance road. After parking, walk to the northern end of the northern parking area, just past the visitor center, to reach the trailhead.

There is no other stream in the redwood forests quite like Prairie Creek—it runs down a long, wide canyon along a ribbon of leafy riparian vegetation, while just back from its banks stand several champion-class redwoods. High up the nearby slope is haunting West Ridge, whose fern-filled forest seems a world apart. Connecting the two

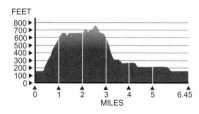

is the rollicking Zig Zag Trail #1, a series of steep switchbacks filled with vistas of the valley below.

The route starts at the main trailhead just north of the Elk Prairie Visitor Center. Descend to a bridge crossing of Prairie Creek, wind through the forest for 0.1 mile, and reach a junction with the Prairie Creek Trail on the right; this is where you will come out near the end of the hike. Continue left to mile 0.15, where you turn right onto the start of the West Ridge Trail. The route runs along the forest floor. It soon turns right and then begins climbing the side of West Ridge on a series of switchbacks. After passing California harebell, you reach the ridgeline at 0.8 mile; the trail now undulates along or near the ridge top as it heads north. There are long-range views of untouched forest to both sides of the trail—large redwoods rise dramatically from a ground cover of thousands of sword ferns. To the left the trees have an especially splendid presence, standing in the shadowed half-light like a group of dignified elders assembled for a silent ceremony.

A sunny opening at 2.0 miles contains Pacific rhododendron, Douglas's iris, and western trillium. Windflower adorns the trailside at 2.65 miles. Just ahead you meet the junction with the Zig Zag Trail #1 on the right. Bear left and continue another 200 feet to reach a park bench just above the trail on the left. The bench faces the canyon that contains the headwaters of Godwood Creek. The lovely view is enhanced by a large rhododendron just downslope. The plaque on the bench is especially apt, capturing the feeling of the forest in a single word: "Forever."

After retracing your route to the Zig Zag #1 junction at 2.75 miles, you turn left and, as the trail's name implies, begin zigging and zagging down a ridge spur toward Prairie Creek, passing Pacific rhododendron and deer fern as you gain increasingly detailed views of the canyon below. At 3.3 miles the Zig Zag ends at the Prairie Creek Trail. Turn right and head downstream, passing large redwoods and beds of deep-green redwood sorrel. You are now in the broad canyon of Prairie Creek. Red alder and bigleaf maple shade the stream, which you cross next to a sediment monitoring station on the right. Look for the large, shiny leaves of stink currant in the creekbed below the bridge.

An L-shaped bridge takes you over Brown Creek at 4.05 miles to a junction with a left-hand spur trail that leads to the Parkway. Continue to the right, passing another monitoring shed and encountering many

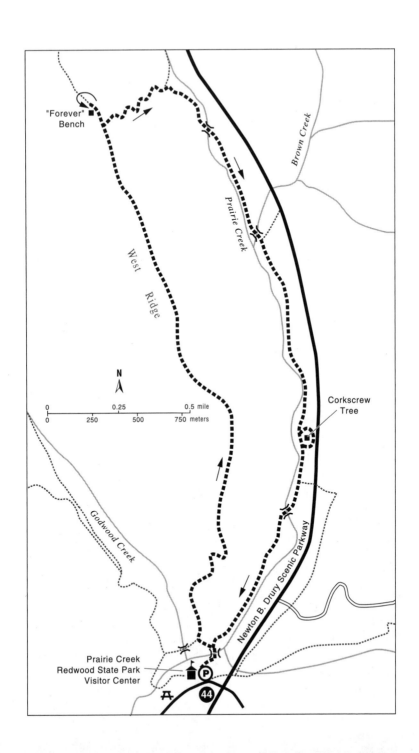

"Forever"
Bench

Brown Creek

Prairie Creek

West Ridge

N

| 0 | 0.25 | 0.5 mile |

| 0 | 250 | 500 | 750 meters |

Corkscrew
Tree

Newton B. Drury Scenic Parkway

Godwood Creek

Prairie Creek
Redwood State Park
Visitor Center

P

44

mossy-trunked bigleaf maples. A junction at 4.55 miles allows you to turn left and stroll 100 feet to the Corkscrew Tree, a collection of twisted trunks that spiral upward together like the enormous braid of some giant's gray hair. A path encircles the tree, allowing you to view the entertaining entwinement from all angles. Ignoring the side trail that leads to the Parkway, complete your circuit of the Corkscrew and return to the Prairie Creek Trail, where you turn left to continue downstream, passing yet more bigleaf maples, including

Looking down Zig Zag Trail #1

one at the trail junction that has arched its trunk over the path and then plunged it into the ground.

Bigleaf maple (*Acer macrophyllum*) justifies its name by producing leaves that measure as much as 14 inches across. The local Yurok Indians used the leaves as a sort of early-day wax paper, placing them between freshly cut salmon fillets. Today the leaves are valued for their aesthetic, rather than practical, appeal. In summer they form a mass of vivid green that illuminates forest otherwise darkened by conifers. In fall the leaves become a nearly incandescent yellow. Aging further, they darken and drop to the ground, providing the trails with a crackly orange carpet. The trunks offer their own artistry, twisting and bending into a thousand different shapes beneath the straight shafts of the surrounding conifers, all the while clothing themselves in a covering of soft, dark green moss that begs to be touched. Pass not too quickly by bigleaf maples, for those who pause beneath them will be enchanted by their manifold charms.

Two sets of stairs at 4.95 miles allow you to walk along part of the trunk of a huge fallen redwood. At 5.2 miles ignore two paths to the left which, in rapid succession, lead to the Parkway. You cross Prairie Creek on a striking wooden bridge, climb a short distance up the hillslope, and then drop to meet the Nature Trail at 6.35 miles. Turn left, crossing Prairie Creek a final time before finishing back at the trailhead.

45. ELK PRAIRIE LOOP

Features ▪	full-length views of several tall redwoods, beautiful Boyes Creek, and a circuit of the northern parks' premier prairie
Distance ▪	2.6 miles round trip
Elevation gain ▪	100 feet
Difficulty ▪	moderate
Open ▪	all year

Driving directions: Drive to mile 0.4 (8.9) of the Newton B. Drury Scenic Parkway at the north end of Elk Prairie. Turn west onto the campground entrance road and go 100 yards to the Elk Prairie Visitor Center. Here you will find two parking areas (no fee), one on each side of the entrance road. After parking, walk to the northern end of the northern parking area, just past the visitor center, to reach the trailhead.

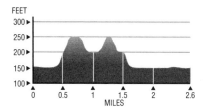

For decades Elk Prairie was *the* place in California to see the native Roosevelt elk. Nowadays, there are other locations where newer herds are often more visible than the somewhat reclusive group that remains here. Nevertheless, the hike around the prairie is filled with other grand views and is well worth the hour or so it takes to complete it.

The route starts at the visitor center parking lot, proceeding eastward next to the entrance road. A sign notes that you are on the Cathedral Trees Trail, but here it serves double duty by also being part of the Elk Prairie Loop. The path runs next to the entrance road for about 75 yards before bending left to drop to the bank of Boyes Creek. A narrow walkway takes you through the creek's culvert beneath the Parkway at 0.1 mile. Steps then rise to a gravel path that continues along the creek. You soon enter a red alder grove and cross Boyes Creek on a substantial timbered bridge. The Foothill Trail forks left at 0.2 mile; go right to a small prairie bordered by a stand of rusty barked redwoods to your left. By cutting across the grass to the far

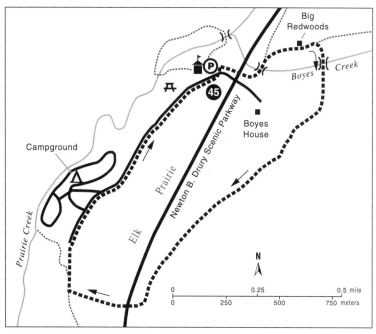

Old camp stove at Elk Prairie Picnic Area

edge of the prairie, photographers may position themselves for a rare full-length view of old-growth redwoods.

You leave the opening and enter a grove of California bay. The trees' aromatic leaves have a nose-twitching astringency that will bring sleepy hikers to instant alertness. Reaching a junction at 0.4 mile, the Cathedral Trees Trail departs to the left (see Hike 46) while you go right, almost immediately recrossing Boyes Creek. Climb a short distance onto the hillslope east of Elk Prairie, passing several large western hemlocks that are followed by some even larger redwoods. After crossing a creeklet filled with skunk cabbage, you come near the edge of the prairie. Here you can view the Boyes House, built by a family that once owned the prairie, and its nearby remnant apple orchard. You may glimpse elk in the grass near the apple trees. Pass around the end of a large redwood log alongside the prairie at 0.85 mile.

After continuing along the base of the redwood-covered hillslope, you drop slightly, turn to the right, cross a boardwalk, and at 1.55 miles reach the Parkway. The trail resumes at a split-rail fence west of the road, running along the southern edge of the prairie. To the left numerous cascara bushes separate you from the more distant conifers, while bracken fern cover much of the open area to the right. At 1.7 miles you meet the Davison Trail, which here follows a section of the old county wagon road (Hike 32). Turn right and follow the roadbed north. To the left at 1.8 miles is a former section of the Elk Prairie Trail that is closed a short distance ahead due to a missing bridge. Continue on the old road-bed, which presently becomes one of the campground roads. Bear right at an intersection and, as you leave the camping area, climb above the road onto the edge of the prairie, where it is both safer and more scenic. Pass a picnic area on the left and cross the road to reach the visitor center.

46. CATHEDRAL TREES–BIG TREE LOOP

Features ▪	cathedral-like clusters of redwoods, an enormous individual tree, and one of the park's finest grove markers
Distance ▪	2.6 miles, loop
Elevation gain ▪	200 feet
Difficulty ▪	moderate
Open ▪	all year

Driving directions: Drive to mile 0.4 (8.9) of the Newton B. Drury Scenic Parkway at the north end of Elk Prairie. Turn west onto the campground entrance road and go 100 yards to the Elk Prairie Visitor Center. Here you will find two parking areas (no fee), one on each side of the entrance road. After parking, walk to the northern end of the northern parking area, just past the visitor center, to reach the trailhead.

No two redwoods look alike, but this hike offers some especially singular specimens, if you count the unique circular groupings called cathedrals. Few trails feature so many scenic spots in as short a distance, which makes this loop a good choice for quickly sampling the splendors of the Prairie Creek park.

Begin on the combined Cathedral Trees Trail–Elk Prairie Loop, which heads east from the trailhead next to the campground access road. Drop from the roadside to pass under the Parkway through the culvert for Boyes Creek, climb briefly into a grove of red alders, and then cross

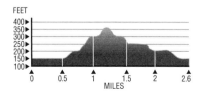

Boyes Creek. Bear right at a junction with the Foothill Trail at 0.2 mile and pass several large redwoods on the left. The trees may be photographed from base to tip by walking right to the far edge of

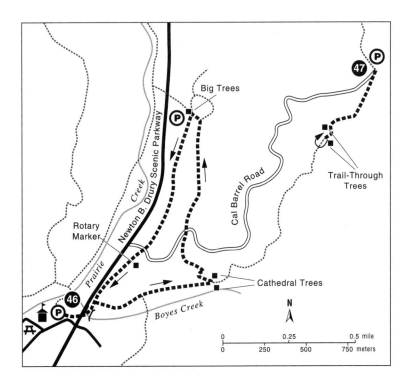

the prairie. You then enter a grove of California bay and reach a junction at 0.4 mile. Turn left, leaving the Elk Prairie Loop and continuing on the Cathedral Trees Trail. The path winds through more California bay and bigleaf maple, next cutting through a thicket of very tall salmonberry. Just past an exceptionally large bay at 0.7 mile on the right is a junction with the Rhododendron Trail, which forks to the right between a pair of cathedral tree groupings. The "cathedrals" are massive circles of tall brown columns—each column is an individual redwood that sprouted off the remains of a central ancestor, and, when combined with their circling cohorts, assumes architectural proportions.

You turn left at the junction. Soon you pass several eye-catching redwoods and then switchback up the hill, seeing California hazel and tanoak before leveling on the end of a ridge. After curving around the contorted roots of a large fallen redwood, you cross Cal Barrel Road at 1.1 miles, picking up the trail diagonally to the left. Ramble across the hillside, dropping to a junction with the Circle Trail at 1.55 miles. Go left to Big Tree, a massive redwood that merits its own protective fence and a sign full of impressive statistics.

From Big Tree go left on the Foothill Trail, following a section of the old county wagon road through California bay and past a parking lot. You cross Cal Barrel Road at 2.1 miles and come to the marker for the Rotary Grove, an attractive stone pillar on which the organization's toothed wheel is carved. Most recent grove markers are made of redwood; earlier ones often featured a bronze plaque embedded in a small boulder. The unusual monument for the Rotary Grove reposes in the forest's half light like a relic from some vanished civilization.

Rotary Grove marker

Continuing through the forested corridor, you complete the loop portion of the hike at 2.4 miles and turn right onto the combined Cathedral Trees–Elk Prairie Trail, perhaps pausing beneath the alders on the Boyes Creek bridge before retracing your steps to the visitor center.

47. TRAIL-THROUGH TREES

Features	▪	a trail that runs through the burned-out centers of not one, but two fire-stricken redwoods
Distance	▪	0.8 mile round trip (longer hike option available)
Elevation gain	▪	50 feet
Difficulty	▪	moderate
Open	▪	all year, except during storms (the Cal Barrel Road access may be closed in wet weather—contact the visitor center for current status)

Driving directions: Take the Newton B. Drury Scenic Parkway to Cal Barrel Road at mile 1.5 (7.8) of the Parkway. Turn east onto

Cal Barrel Road and follow it 1.9 miles to its end at a parking area for the Rhododendron Trail.

While more fire resistant than most trees, redwoods nonetheless sometimes suffer flame-induced damage to their interiors. This short, hillside trek takes hikers through a pair of large, burned-out specimens.

From the parking area, ramble 50 yards back down Cal Barrel Road to a sign for the Rhododendron–Cathedral Trees–Elk Prairie trails. (See map on page 176.) Many years ago the road led to the top of the ridge, where the California Barrel Company had one of its logging camps. CABCO, as the company was called, cut mainly Sitka spruce for lightweight wooden crates and barrels. For years its mill in Arcata was the city's largest employer.

Departing the road, you follow the trail uphill, immediately passing beneath two large fallen redwoods before crossing a small creekbed and cutting along the forested hillside. A short uphill switchback brings you to a large patch of windflower, along with Douglas's iris and California hazel at mile 0.1.

Windflower (*Anemone deltoidea*) is a demure flower of the deep forest, often congregating in small colonies that brighten the darkness with patches of soft whiteness. The coloring comes not from the windflower's petals, of which it has none, but from its sepals, which are white instead of the usual green. These perch upon a slender stalk several inches above a whorl of three pointed leaflets that lie close to the ground. The plant's name derives from a folklore belief that this anemone opens only when the wind is blowing, a fiction that will be exposed whenever anyone passes this pretty flower on a calm day.

Your route then descends on switchbacks before leveling. Another short drop is followed by a brief climb to Trail-Through Tree #1 at 0.3 mile, a large, fire-blasted redwood with a small opening in its side. The trail takes you through the opening into the center of what proves to be a "chimney" tree—these are redwoods that have had their interiors burned away, so that someone inside the trunk can see daylight through the opening at the tree's top.

After passing clintonia and tiger lily you switchback downhill to reach Trail-Through Tree #2, which is actually a pair of joined redwoods, between which the path passes via a burned-out

Trail-Through Tree #1

connecting section. Here, at 0.4 mile, your route reverses to return to the parking area.

For a longer hike: Continue downhill past Trail-Through Tree #2, traversing a remote section of redwood forest. Eventually cross under and through a jumble of large, downed redwoods and climb uphill to a junction; here you turn right, ascending 75 feet to meet Cal Barrel Road. Turn right onto the road and follow it uphill to the parking lot. This extension adds 2.5 miles to the hike.

48. PRAIRIE CREEK RHODODENDRON

Features ▪	high-elevation redwoods and numerous hillside rhododendrons
Distance ▪	2.3 miles round trip (longer options available)
Elevation gain ▪	150 feet
Difficulty ▪	moderate
Open ▪	all year, except during storms (the Cal Barrel Road access may be closed in wet weather—contact the visitor center for current status)

Driving directions: Take the Newton B. Drury Scenic Parkway to Cal Barrel Road at mile 1.5 (7.8) of the Parkway. Turn east onto Cal Barrel Road and follow it 1.9 miles to its end at a parking area for the Rhododendron Trail.

Pacific rhododendrons are the most eye-catching flowering shrub in the redwood forest, and a spring hike on this ridge-side trail showcases them at their best.

The hike begins at the north edge of the parking area on a segment of the Rhododendron Trail, named for the route's signature flower. The Pacific, or California, rhododendron (*Rhododendron macrophylum*) is a large and seasonally spectacular shrub. Growing up to 25 feet tall in the depths of coastal forests, come May and June it covers itself with pinkish rose flower clusters that are often 6 inches or more in diameter. To see them softly glowing through the morning mists of a redwood-covered hillside is one of the signal events of spring, and one of the best places to experience them is along this trail.

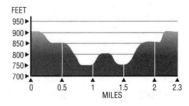

The route immediately descends through a mixed forest of Douglas-fir, western hemlock,

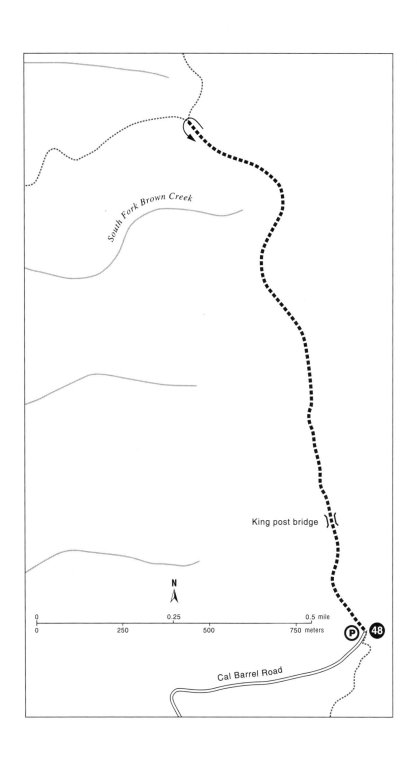

South Fork Brown Creek

King post bridge)=(

N

| 0 | | 0.25 | | 0.5 mile |
0   250   500   750 meters

P 48

Cal Barrel Road

and redwood. The path soon levels and undulates across the side of East Ridge, with Prairie Creek far below in the canyon to the left and the ridge top lost in the forest upslope to the right. Redwoods rise rigidly from the hillside like quills on the back of an immense porcupine. After crossing three small bridges the trail reaches a larger, king post bridge at 0.25 mile where many deer ferns fill the streambed. A series of colorful forest flowers ensues, including clintonia, Pacific rhododendron, and tiger lily. At 0.8 mile the trail switchbacks downhill, crosses a rock-strewn stream and then climbs gently to a left-hand junction with the South Fork Trail at 1.15 miles. Your hike reverses course here to Cal Barrel Road.

For a longer hike: At the junction with the South Fork Trail, two options are available: 1) a left turn onto the South Fork Trail allows you to add most of the Brown Creek Loop (Hike 49), returning to the junction in 2.7 miles; or 2) bearing right and continuing on the Rhododendron Trail will take you to the Brown Creek Trail in 1.2 miles, from where you can double back to the junction for a 2.4-mile addition.

Pacific rhododendron along its namesake trail

49. BROWN CREEK LOOP

Features	▪ a pair of pretty creek canyons, hillside wildflowers, and the chance to view a set of nearly forgotten monuments
Distance	▪ 3.6 miles round trip
Elevation gain	▪ 600 feet
Difficulty	▪ moderate
Open	▪ all year

Driving directions: Drive to mile 2.9 (6.4) of the Newton B. Drury Scenic Parkway. The trailhead is on the eastern side of the road.

The two forks of Brown Creek and the ridge between them are the setting for this scenic loop. History seekers will find a special attraction along the way—a 21-tree salute to early day foresters.

Our hike begins at a marked trailhead on the east side of the Parkway. The path winds through large trees, with Brown Creek nearby on the left. At a junction at 0.2 mile the Foothill Trail branches right. Bear left, passing several shattered redwoods that lie in disarray upon the hillslope to the right. The path is fringed with wildflowers, including Smith's fairybell, northern inside-out flower, and trail plant. You soon cross South Fork Creek on a one-rail bridge. The path forks on the far side of the bridge; to the right is the South Fork Trail, while to the left is your route, the Brown Creek Trail. Follow this along the hillslope and then cross Brown Creek at 0.5 mile. Go upstream into the redwood-filled canyon.

A right-hand side trail at 0.8 mile drops to a bridge across Brown Creek. On the far side is the Carl Alwin Schenck Grove, dedicated to the founder of the Biltmore School of Forestry, the first of its kind in the United States. The grove loop trail passes a series of twenty-one concrete commemorative markers, each originally placed in front of a giant redwood, but over time some of the grove's trees have fallen, often on the markers.

The trail continues past the Schenck Grove to the Frederick Law Olmstead Grove, which honors the landscape architect who

conducted the survey that served as the basis for the California State
Parks system. The route then cuts across the hillslope before arriving
at an intersection with the Rhododendron Trail at 1.4 miles. Turn
right, crossing Brown Creek on a wooden bridge and then climbing
along the side of East Ridge. Watch for tiger lily at the switchbacks.
Since you are on the Rhododendron Trail, also expect to see some of
its namesake flowers.

Tiger lily (*Lilium columbianum*) is one of the most colorful flowers

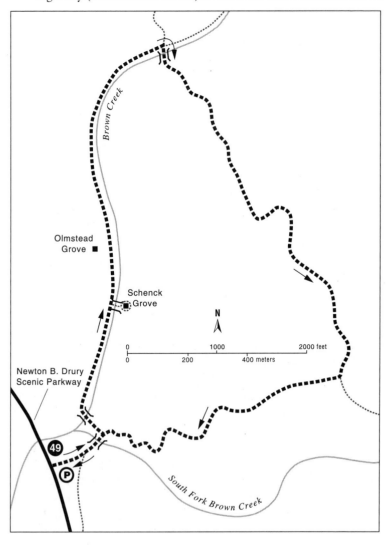

Tiger lilies

of the redwood forest. It grows on a stalk that is usually 2–3 feet tall, from which dangle bright yellow-orange flowers, their recurved (bent back) petals freckled with dozens of tiny dark spots and their pollen-rich stamens arranged parallel to one another in tight clusters. Tiger lilies like a bit of sunlight, so they are found most readily along roads and trails rather than in deep forest.

The route continues along the hillslope until it reaches a junction with the South Fork Trail at 2.6 miles. The way left leads along the route for Hike 48. Turn right, heading west onto a ridge spur past more lilies before dropping on switchbacks to meet the Brown Creek Trail at 3.4 miles. A left turn here retraces the first stage of your hike, bearing right at the junction with the Foothill Trail and returning to the trailhead.

50. LITTLE CREEK

Features	■	interesting plants and a peaceful hillside overlook
Distance	■	0.5 mile round trip
Elevation gain	■	100 feet
Difficulty	■	easy
Open	■	all year

Driving directions: Drive to mile 5.9 (3.4) of the Newton B. Drury Scenic Parkway. The trailhead is on the eastern side of the road.

Tired of driving? This little trail above Little Creek will stretch tight muscles and soothe your eyes with forest greenery.

Lovely Little Creek once had a trail of many boardwalks and bridges that crisscrossed the boggy, shrub-filled stream. Now, only

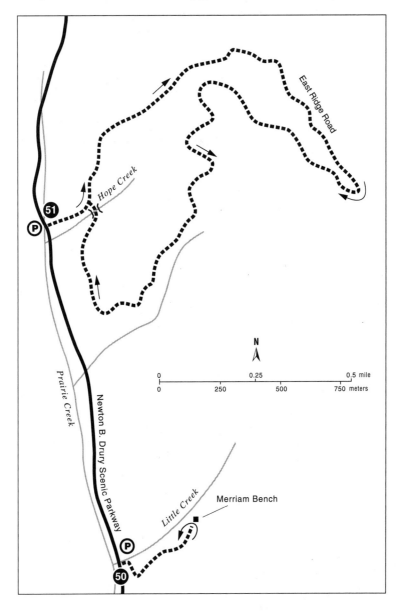

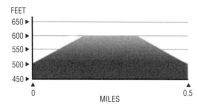

the sign for that route remains. The new trail starts to the right of the old marker, where you promptly climb the southern side of the creek canyon, switchbacking in 50 yards to head east. A mixed forest of Douglas-fir, Sitka spruce, and coast redwood shade the slope, while toothed monkeyflower, fringe cup, and deer fern grow by the trail. After crossing a small rivulet at 0.15 mile, you pass over a larger stream. Here you find clasping twisted stalk, a flower as unusual as its name.

The stems of clasping twisted stalk (*Streptopus amplexifolius*) display a series of dark green, oval leaves. Each leaf encircles, or "clasps," the stem, which accounts for half of the plant's name. The other half derives from its pedicel, the thin stalk that connects the bell-like flower to the stem. Each pedicel has a right-angle crimp, or "twist," in it, as if Mother Nature had been busy with a pair of needle-nose pliers. To see this handiwork you have to twist a bit yourself, bending low to look underneath the sheltering leaves. By late summer the flowers have transformed themselves into shiny red fruit.

Stream crossing on split redwood bridge

The trail ends at a handsome wooden bench dedicated to Frank Finlay Merriam, governor of California from 1934 to 1939, and, as the plaque helpfully adds, also a realtor. The bench is a perfect place to rest for a few minutes and contemplate some wonderful real estate—the delightful canyon of Little Creek. Then it is about-face and downward to the trailhead at 0.5 mile.

51. HOPE CREEK–TEN TAYPO LOOP

Features ▪	lots of rhododendrons, a stand of western hemlocks, and two lovely stream canyons
Distance ▪	3.75 miles, loop
Elevation gain ▪	500 feet
Difficulty ▪	strenuous
Open ▪	all year

Driving directions: Drive to mile 6.8 (2.5) of the Newton B. Drury Scenic Parkway. The trailhead is on the east side of the road.

This ridge-reaching route combines two park trails with an abandoned section of East Ridge Road, offering both a good workout and varied terrain. It is a perfect half-day hike for those who crave some seclusion with their scenery.

The trail climbs uphill from a pullout alongside the Parkway. (See map on page 186.) Soon the route undulates across the hillside, passing mock azalea and Pacific rhododendron. At 0.3 mile the trail divides. To the right is the Ten Taypo Trail, which eventually concludes the loop portion of the hike. Go left, continuing on the Hope Creek Trail as it ascends its namesake canyon, passing tanoak, Columbia lily, and redwood violet before cutting through the trunk of a medium-size redwood. The trail reaches a stand of young western hemlock at 0.8 mile, which has colonized a burned-over section of the forest.

Western hemlock (*Tsuga heterophylla*) is—along with coast redwood, Douglas-fir, and Sitka spruce—one of the four commonly seen conifers in the parks. The other three are all much larger trees (the tallest recorded

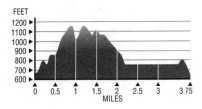

Bridge over Hope Creek

hemlock is only 174 feet tall), and so the smaller Tsuga usually assumes the role of an understory plant, aided in this by its tolerance of shade. Western hemlock is used for lumber and pulp, and also for items formerly made from redwood, such as poles, pilings, and railroad ties. When left to its own devices, western hemlock often fills the lower forest with a soft green fog—its short, overlapping needles growing densely on its twigs, creating a concentration of foliage unmatched by any of its companion conifers.

After crossing a ridgeline, the route drops past large redwoods and arrives at what was once East Ridge Road at 1.05 miles. The way left is now blocked, and the trail turns right to follow the roadbed uphill. Years ago the road provided access to ridge-top redwood groves and connected several hiking routes that came up from Prairie Creek. When the Park Bypass was built, the highway cut through sections of East Ridge Road, leaving only short remnants, like this one, and isolating other sections of the ridgeline.

Follow the roadbed past a scattering of windflower and onto the top of East Ridge. Soon the road drops over the far side of the ridgeline, where Pacific rhododendron and Columbia lily brighten the way in spring. At 1.5 miles the route leaves the roadbed, turning right and descending on the Ten Taypo Trail. Hike along the top of the upper Ten Taypo drainage, gradually dropping into the canyon after the trail turns west. The path stays far above the creek, running along the hillside and finally rounding the end of the ridgeline at 3.2 miles, where the route bends into the canyon of Hope Creek, crossing the stream on a sinuous S-shaped bridge and then climbing to reach a junction with the Hope Creek Trail at 3.45 miles. Turn left here and retrace the first section of the hike.

52. OSSAGON ROCKS

Features	■	lots of alder thickets, possibly an elk herd, and the dark triangles of the Ossagon Rocks jutting up from the wide, pale beach
Distance	■	4.8 miles round trip
Elevation gain	■	700 feet
Difficulty	■	strenuous
Open	■	all year

Driving Directions: Drive to mile 6.8 (2.5) of the Newton B. Drury Scenic Parkway. The trailhead is on the west side of the road.

You'll only see a few redwoods on this forest-to-beach hike, but lovely groves of alders, the dramatic Ossagon Rocks, and the chance to encounter a roaming elk herd are more than enough to compensate. Be prepared for a stiff climb on your return from the beach.

Leave the west side of the parking area near a large Sitka spruce, crossing Prairie Creek in 50 feet. The route is uphill, passing through salmonberry and deer fern as you climb out of the canyon. At 0.2 mile you reach the ridgeline, which you follow until 0.4 mile, where you meet the old Ossagon Road. The way right is blocked by a park bench, and you turn left onto the aging roadbed (cars were actually allowed on this steep, narrow route until the 1960s). Soon you drop downhill through mixed forest, the sound of the surf rumbling in the distance.

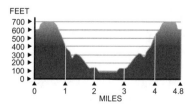

Ossagon Rocks

Red alder cover the slopes near the road, their leaves providing welcome shade in summer.

The route continues to drop until mile 1.25, where it crosses the north fork of Ossagon Creek on a wooden bridge. A dam upstream once impounded water for the Eureka Placer Mining Company, which attempted, with scant success, to wash profitable amounts of ore from the section of creek downstream from the bridge. The trail then rises to cut across the hillside above the creek, eventually dropping through more alders until you reach a shaded flat at the mouth of Ossagon Creek at 1.8 miles. You now follow the creek past the Ossagon Backpack Camp on the right, bearing left at junctions with spur trails to the camp sites. Soon you cross the bridgeless creek on several wooden planks and meet the Coastal Trail at 1.9 miles. The way left leads to Fern Canyon and the Gold Bluffs Beach Road. (This route may be inundated at its near end during the rainy season.) Turn right, following the Coastal Trail toward the beach. A bridge takes you over a marshy area at 2.0 miles, and you then move into sand dunes. Just ahead the trail forks; left leads to the beach while right takes you through the dune area. Go right, aiming, when the trail grows faint, for the now-visible Ossagon Rocks. At 2.4 miles you reach the main cluster of four large rocks, dark gray projections whose tips point piercingly skyward. The rocks hold deep significance for the local Yurok Indians, so please walk among them with respect.

The route turns back here, but it is easy to yield to the temptations provided by the nearby ocean to the west and the seasonal lagoon to the east. The dune area and wetlands may offer their own attraction—a roaming herd of Roosevelt elk that browse on the area's varied vegetation. Taking the most direct course back, however, will

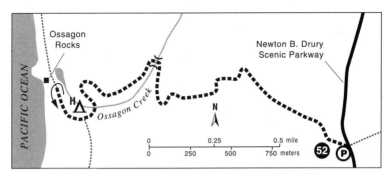

return you to the trailhead at 4.8 miles, after a steep climb up and over the ridge.

53. CROTHERS COVE

Features	■	a placid lagoon, dramatic rocks, and a stretch of isolated beach
Distance	■	1.8 miles round trip
Elevation gain	■	550 feet
Difficulty	■	strenuous
Open	■	all year

Driving directions: Drive to mile 8.3 (1.0) of the Newton B. Drury Parkway. Turn west onto Coastal Drive and drive 1.1 miles to the trailhead on the west side of the road.

This route could well be called "the hike of the misnamed places," for it goes past two (or possibly three) historic sites whose spellings have become garbled over the years. Perhaps someone will consider, after completing this dramatic trek, petitioning the Board of Geographic Names to set aright what has gone amiss.

The approach to the trailhead takes you along a short stretch of Coastal Drive, a former stretch of Highway 101 that is now a park road.

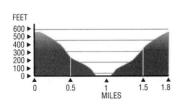

An exceptionally fine row of redwoods at the Ada Fenimore Bock Grove at 0.7 mile shows what has been lost by the rerouting of the highway.

Leave the west side of Coastal Drive by descending on the Coastal

Trail towards the ocean. In 30 feet you cross the bed of the county wagon road (see Hikes 32 and 37). Some 3 miles to the north Coastal Drive runs along the wagon road's old route, which it follows toward the road's former ferry crossing at the Klamath. Just beyond the wagon road remnant the path picks up another roadbed and begins following it downhill. Look to the left for masses of Smith's fairy bell. The road once led to the summer home of Eureka newspaper publisher J. H. Crothers. The coastal indentation below his bluff-top house site appears on trail signs and maps as Carruthers Cove, the result of a careless misspelling that would have cost the proofreader in Crothers' newsroom his job.

Small to medium Sitka spruce cover much of the descending trail, which makes a sharp left turn at 0.25 mile and then heads southwest. A right turn at 0.6 mile allows you to follow the canyon of Johnson Creek to the left. Someone, perhaps a parsimonious map publisher, has created the second misspelling on the route, for he or she omitted the "t" from Anthony Dale and Julia Sheridan Johnston's last name. The Johnstons settled here in 1851 and developed a ranch and well-known traveler's stopping place. Anthony used water from the creek for his Amony Placer Mine, which probably contains yet another misspelling—a failed attempt to decipher a handwritten rendering of "Anthony." On the hillside across the creek is a remnant of the ditch that carried water to the mine. Reaching the site is both difficult and possibly dangerous and is not recommended.

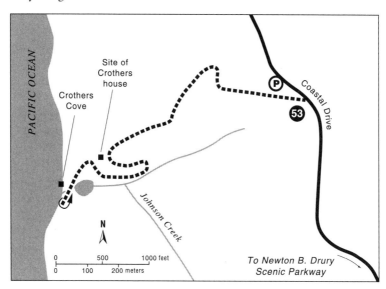

Crothers Cove rocks and beach

The trail leaves the roadbed just ahead. The road to the right is now heavily overgrown and difficult to discern, but it once led a short distance to the Crothers house. During World War II the building, by then deserted, was used by the Coast Guard as quarters for their beach patrol.

The route travels along the unstable slope below the house site; the trail here may be in poor condition due to slumping and sliding. Bend right, crossing the front of the bluff, and then turn left, passing through a thicket of red alder, willow, and salmonberry. At 0.8 mile you emerge onto the beach. Go left, heading towards a large craggy rock that shelters a small lagoon. Look for great blue herons, egrets, and kingfishers. In earlier days the ocean came all the way to the rock, forming the misnamed cove. Now a broad beach lies west of the lagoon, which is fed by Johnson Creek. Skirt the lagoon, passing sea rocket, beach evening primrose, and pink sand verbena, and proceed along the beach to where you have a full view of the coastal side of the rock. To the south a group of offshore rocks beckons, as does the beach to the north. You may want to roam in either direction, but the official hike reverses course here, climbing steeply on the way back to the trailhead, which you reach at 1.8 miles.

DEL NORTE COAST REDWOODS STATE PARK

Alone among the parks covered by this book, Del Norte (the "e" is silent) Coast Redwoods is most noted for its steep, forested mountain slopes rather than the redwood-filled flats for which the others are famed. Starting at a rocky shoreline, the lands of Del Norte Coast rise on dramatic diagonals to reach a heavily timbered ridge top along which Highway 101 twists and turns. Eastward, the park contains another great slope, this one plunging to the bottom of the canyon of Mill Creek, a place once packed with old-growth giants that were logged in the 1920s and 1930s.

While the other state parks each have an alternate driving route that offers a respite from the fast pace of Highway 101, Del Norte Coast again differs—it has an older version of the highway, but it is only open to hikers and cyclists, and part of it, which once cut its way across the coastal cliffs, has inconveniently slid into the ocean. Yet this only adds to the allure of Del Norte Coast—the park that dares to be different—and that therefore offers hikers a unique experience.

In 1925 a 157-acre grove of hillside redwoods, dedicated to Henry Solon Graves, the former chief forester of the U. S. Forest Service, became the first unit in Del Norte Coast Redwoods State Park. The grove was situated along the original route of the Redwood Highway, a road that would reach completion the following year when the Douglas Memorial Bridge finally replaced the ferry across the Klamath River.

The park grew rapidly, so that by 1931 it contained over 2300 acres. The previous year, an average of 1550 motorists came through every day on the Redwood Highway, but gravity was having a grave effect on the road—landslides along the cliff-clinging section of the route were frequent, creating the very real possibility that sections of its thin ribbon of pavement would soon plunge into the sea. As a result, 9.5 miles of the highway were rerouted in 1934 up onto the ridge, very near, in fact, to the forty-year-old route of the Arcata to Crescent City wagon road. The revised roadway was not only more stable but also straighter; what had been a twisting course of some 239 curves now had only thirty-nine bends in it. Such improvements, however, came at a price, for the new section of highway no longer offered the thrilling proximity to the sea and part of it went through an area where Hobbs, Wall & Company had recently logged the old-growth forest. In time, however, a new generation of trees began to rise above the Redwood Highway, while the park converted part of the cutover canyon to the east into its Mill Creek Campground—now a secluded and highly scenic spot. The state parks' recent acquisition of some 25,000 acres of previously logged forestland downcanyon from the campground promises even more for the future, since the purchase will link the Del Norte Coast park to Jedediah Smith Redwoods and to lands owned by Redwood National Park.

Del Norte Coast Redwoods State Park has no visitor center. The 145-site Mill Creek Campground is reached by a 2-mile access road from Highway 101, along which an entrance station assesses day-use and camping fees. The campground is open from April 1 through October 1. A locked gate near Highway 101 prevents use of the access road the rest of the year.

This book covers four hikes that are located in the park. Driving directions along Highway 101 are given from Wilson Creek Road to the south, with distances from the north, which are computed from the intersection of the highway and Enderts Beach Road, given in parentheses. *Note: to reach the trailhead for Hike 57 you must pay a day-use fee.*

54. DEL NORTE COAST RHODODENDRON

Features ■	steep-sided, fern-filled canyons and a profusion of Pacific rhododendrons
Distance ■	5.4 miles round trip (longer option available)
Elevation gain ■	200 feet
Difficulty ■	strenuous
Open ■	all year

Driving directions: Take Highway 101 to a point 2.9 miles north of Wilson Creek Road (8.4 miles south of Enderts Beach Road); the trailhead is on the east side of the highway. *Warning: when approaching the trailhead parking area from the north, use extreme caution when crossing the northbound lane of Highway 101.*

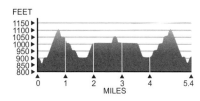

If you want a satisfying spring hike, come here in late May or early June and behold a rampage of rhododendrons that will equal any the parks have to offer. You'll also be awed by the spellbinding array of sword ferns that covers the canyonsides.

Start on what is known as the DeMartin section of the Coastal Trail. The route drops immediately into a redwood forest, passing through two large trees before making a switchback and arriving at a railed bridge. Salmonberry, lady fern, and mock azalea cluster near the bridge, while to its right an immense Sitka spruce rises above and overshadows a shattered remnant of a smaller tree on the left. The full-sized spruce is clothed in a skirt of leather ferns near its base, while the shattered tree is nearly covered with the ferns.

Second in grandeur only to the redwood among coastal conifers is the Sitka spruce (*Picea sitchensis*), which can be both tall (up to 320 feet) and thick (up to 16 feet in diameter). When close to the briny breezes off the Pacific, the coast redwood, despite its name, yields in prominence to the Sitka spruce, which thrives where the salt-sensitive *Sequoia sempervirens* becomes stunted. Near the ocean you will see the most massive spruces, their flaky, light gray bark like a set of small shingles cladding a gigantic tower. Spruce is a lightweight but strong wood, used in boat building and for piano and violin soundboards, but its greatest utility occurs when it is left alone, adding its sublime presence to the forest.

Leaving the bridge, hike upward on switchbacks until the trail levels and heads east at 0.6 mile, passing redwood sorrel, five-finger fern, tiger lily, and baneberry. You also begin encountering Pacific rhododendron, which will become more prolific as you progress. To the left the canyonside drops away into shadowy greenness, the steep slopes covered with redwood-shaded sword fern. The trail then descends gradually along the slope. A canyon indentation at 1.3 miles ends in a saddle to the right that promises a view of the ocean from the ridgeline, but the intervening vegetation is far too thick to provide easy passage.

As the trail begins rising again, rhododendrons return in force at 1.75 miles, continuing so for a quarter mile. An uphill pitch culminates in your cresting the ridgeline at 2.7 miles. Here the trail begins its long descent to Wilson Creek and the old DeMartin Ranch. The

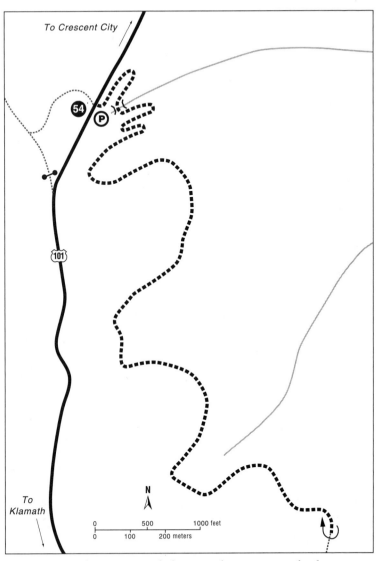

To Crescent City

54

P

101

To
Klamath

N

0   500   1000 feet
0   100   200 meters

hike, however, has gone south far enough, so you turn back to return
to the trailhead.

    For a longer hike: If you have arranged a car shuttle, you can
continue south from the ridgeline, reaching a junction in a clearing:
right takes you out to Highway 101 on a park access road, meeting the

Opposite: *Sitka spruce with leather ferns*

highway 1.5 miles north of Wilson Creek Road; left continues on the DeMartin Coastal Trail, passing the DeMartin Backpack Camp and then dropping steeply to the trailhead at the north end of the Wilson Creek bridge.

55. DAMNATION CREEK

Features ■	hillside forests and a spectacular overlook of both the ocean and nearby coastal cliffs
Distance ■	4.2 miles round trip
Elevation Change ■	1000 feet
Difficulty ■	strenuous
Open ■	all year

Driving directions: Take Highway 101 to a point 3.3 miles north of Wilson Creek Road (8 miles south of Enderts Beach Road). The trailhead is on the western side of the highway. *Warning: when approaching the trailhead parking area from the south, use extreme care when crossing the southbound lane of Highway 101.*

Damnation Creek was called *Shaaxuutchudun* ("the big one") by the local Tolowa Indians. How it received its current name is a mystery, although anyone who has had to climb out of its deep canyon on a hot day may want to utter at least a small oath while laboring to reach the ridge. If you are in good physical condition, though, do not let the 1000-foot elevation change deter you; the trail is charming and the beachside bluff top at its end offers postcard-perfect views up and down the coast.

The trail rises westward from the parking area, passing large redwoods and numerous Pacific rhododendrons. You soon pick up the track of the old county wagon road, built in the 1890s, which the path follows until mile 0.2. Here the trail cuts uphill to the left, while the roadbed continues to the right. In a few hundred feet you reach the ridge top and begin your descent to the coast. Look for a redwood on the left with a large burl covered with dark green leather ferns.

A path branches left at 0.6 mile; continue right to where your route crosses a long-abandoned section of Highway 101 (see Hike 56). The trail now runs out onto

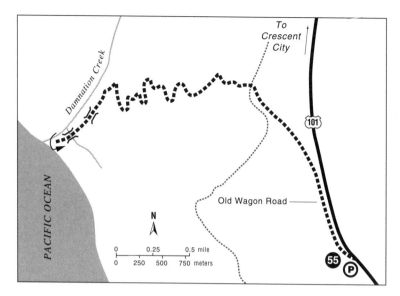

a ridge spur before dropping down the canyonside of Damnation Creek on a series of switchbacks. Deer fern and both Smith's and Hooker's fairybells line stretches of the path.

Hooker's fairybell (*Disporum hookeri*) and Smith's fairybell (*Disporum smithii*) may appear to be mere collections of dark green leaves, but they are worth a closer look. Hanging beneath the foliage are numerous pale, bell-shaped flowers that seem to glow like tiny spots of light in the forest shadows. Their delicate petals and soft color form a sharp contrast to the massive, dark-hued trunks of the nearby trees. Two ways to tell the species apart: 1) the creamy white bell on the Smith's is longer and more cylindrical than that of the greenish white, funnel-shaped Hooker's; 2) the leaves on the Smith's are smooth while those on the Hooker's are hairy (think S = Smith's = smooth; H = Hooker's = hairy).

As the trail nears the coast, Sitka spruce and Douglas-fir begin to replace the redwoods, which react unfavorably to salt-laden air. Bigleaf maple and red alder, moistened by the proximity of the creek, appear near the trail at 1.8 mile. The route then levels, crosses two side streams on handsome king post bridges, and rises to an open headland at 2.1 miles. Here a profusion of plant life covers the bluff top—angelica, yarrow, mission bells, cow parsnip, and Douglas's iris. There are stunning views of the ocean, offshore rocks, and dramatic coastline cliffs, in addition to the rocky mouth of Damnation Creek. A path leads down to a

Beach at mouth of Damnation Creek

beach at the base of the cliffs, but it is in dangerously poor condition and cannot be recommended. The hike therefore reverses course at the bluff top, returning, after an endorphin-producing climb, to the trailhead.

56. OLD HIGHWAY 101 NORTH

Features ■	a haunting stretch of long-abandoned roadway and a row of stately redwoods
Distance ■	5.1 miles round trip (longer hike options available)
Elevation gain ■	300 feet
Difficulty ■	strenuous
Open ■	all year

Driving directions: Take Highway 101 to a point 3.3 miles north of Wilson Creek Road (8.4 miles south of Enderts Beach Road). The trailhead is on the west side of the highway. ***Warning:*** *when* *approaching the trailhead parking area from the south, use extreme care when crossing the southbound lane of Highway 101.*

Want to travel back to the 1920s? You can get there by stepping onto the aging pavement of this hiking route, which travels along what was once a scenic stretch of the original Redwood Highway.

While traversing Del Norte Coast Redwoods State Park, the first version of the Redwood Highway followed a lower, more westerly course than today's 101. This brought it through prime groves of hillside redwoods and also out to the coast, where it ran across the open cliff side hundreds of feet above the ocean. Unfortunately, the spectacular northern section of roadway soon started slipping into the sea, so in the early 1930s the park's entire stretch of highway was rerouted eastward, much of it running along the more stable but less scenic ridge top. The southern end of the abandoned highway and a small part that remains at the northern end have been converted into part of the Coastal Trail. This hike takes you along a redwood-shaded sampling of the southern section.

You begin by leaving the parking area on the Damnation Creek Trail (see Hike 55). At 0.2 mile this path temporarily follows the route of the first road through the area. Opened in 1894, it was officially known as the Crescent City to Klamath River Wagon Road, although it would take another four years of improvements before wagons and stages could easily travel the route. At the Klamath River ferry it connected with another section of wagon road that went all the way to Humboldt Bay. The entire road was replaced in the 1920s by the first version of the Redwood Highway, which lies just over the ridge ahead.

You meet the all-but-forgotten highway at 0.6 mile. Here you depart the Damnation Creek Trail as you turn right and head north, treading upon a covering of redwood duff that now obscures the Redwood Highway's roadbed. An old black-and-white road marker at mile 0.8 recalls the route's former status, as do occasional glimpses of aging pavement and faded white line. Just ahead are tiger lily and the smaller but also colorful toothed monkey-flower. The road drops gradually, hugging the redwood-filled hillside. The trees are especially large at about 1.9 miles. A row of stobbers—short wooden posts about a foot high—on the left at 2.3 miles comes just before the

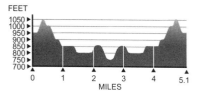

FEET

1050 ►
1000 ►
950 ►
900 ►
850 ►
800 ►
750 ►
700 ►

0   1   2   3   4   5.1
MILES

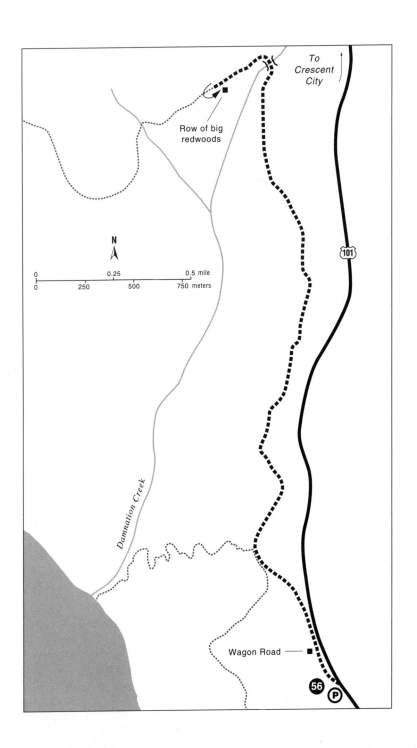

To
Crescent
City

Row of big
redwoods

N

| 0 | | 0.25 | | 0.5 mile |
| 0 | 250 | | 500 | 750 meters |

101

Damnation Creek

Wagon Road

56 P

trail temporarily leaves the road-bed to cross Damnation Creek on a narrow wooden bridge. Where the highway bridge once stood is now an enlarged chasm, eroded over the decades by—damna-tion!—the waters of the creek.

Soon the route regains the roadway and begins a gentle climb uphill. A magnificent row of dark-ened redwoods, their lower trunks scorched by some long-ago fire, stand like monumental columns along the left side of the roadbed. Decades ago, when the highway here was so briefly open, trucks and autos that would now be museum pieces maneuvered past these mas-sive trees, claiming passage in the name of progress. Now no vehicle larger than a mountain bike comes this way, but the trees remain, im-passive in the face of such intima-tions of impermanence.

Old Redwood Highway road marker

After perhaps thus contem-plating the effects of time, you may notice that your watch indicates the rapid progress of the day. Here is a perfect place to change direc-tion and begin your return to the trailhead at 4.7 miles.

For a longer hike: You can walk farther in either direction along the old highway. To the north you can continue past the turnaround point, cutting across the rest of the drainage of Damnation Creek, even-tually crossing over to the coastal side of the ridge and perhaps catching a glimpse of the sea. The Coastal Trail then leaves the old highway to travel overland. It continues north all the way to Enderts Beach Road (see Hike 38) just a few miles south of Crescent City. Hiking the entire route normally requires a car shuttle. To the south you can travel be-yond the intersection with the Damnation Creek Trail, passing the marker for the Henry Solon Graves Grove before reaching the old road's end at modern-day Highway 101. From there you return to the Dam-nation Creek Trail and take it east, over the ridge, to the trailhead.

57. TRESTLE-SKYLINE LOOP

Features	▪	remnants of an old logging operation, lovely Mill Creek, and foliage-filled side canyons
Distance	▪	3.1 miles, loop
Elevation change	▪	400 feet
Difficulty	▪	moderate
Open	▪	when the Mill Creek Campground is in operation—currently April 1 through October 1

Driving directions: Take Highway 101 to the access road for the Mill Creek Campground, 7.6 miles north of Wilson Creek Road (3.7 miles south of Enderts Beach Road). Turn east onto the access road and take it 2 miles downhill to the campground, passing the entrance station midway along the route. Turn left when you reach the intersection at the base of the grade and immediately cross Mill Creek on a bridge. The trailhead is at the northeast corner of the bridge. *Note: to drive to the trailhead you must pay a day-use fee.*

This hike combines the Trestle and Saddler Skyline Trails into a creek-crossing, hillside-climbing loop that takes you past vestiges of an early-day logging operation. During the early decades of the twentieth century the canyon was owned, and its redwoods cut, by Hobbs, Wall & Company, Del Norte County's premier timber operation. Hobbs, Wall & Company had a mill in Crescent City and ran its own rail line, known as the Del Norte Southern, along and over the first ridge east of town and down into Mill Creek. A short distance downstream from the campground the company built what should have been known as Camp 13, but which, due to the superstition of the loggers, was called Camp 12-2. The rail line continued up the canyon to a point south of the campground. To bring logs down from the ridge where Highway 101 now runs, a system of railed "inclines" was built so that railcars running on tracks along the ridge could be lowered crosswise to the canyon floor. A crew

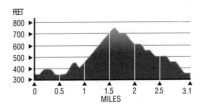

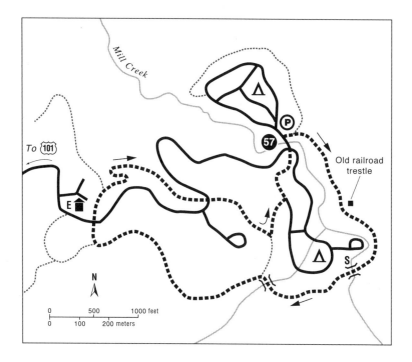

of 165 workers called the camp home, and the results of their labors can still be seen along the route of the hike—a forest of second-growth redwood now some seventy to eighty years old, speckled by the decaying stumps of what became material for the Hobbs, Wall & Company mill.

The route begins on the Trestle Loop, following Mill Creek upstream through bigleaf maple, red alder, and coast red elderberry. In 100 feet go right at a junction with the Alder Basin Trail, passing large stumps on the hillside and switchbacking uphill until the path levels at 0.1 mile. The trail narrows; use caution. Vine maple, tanoak, California hazel, and Pacific rhododendron grow in the understory, while closer to ground California harebell and Bolander's phacelia thrive. A rusty cable from the Hobbs, Wall & Company days reposes on the ground at 0.3 mile, after which the trail drops to cross a creeklet on a sturdy wooden bridge. To the left the keen-eyed can discern the rotting posts of the nearly vanished railroad trestle that gave the trail its name. The route then climbs briefly and crosses the old railbed, running parallel to it for a short distance and then on top of it. The trail is partially corduroyed with trestles that have remained in place. At 0.5 mile the path bends

Mill Creek

right and leaves the railbed behind.

The trail crosses Mill Creek at 0.65 mile on a summer bridge, turns right to climb the hillside, and then follows the creek downstream. Soon the path becomes challenging—steep, narrow, and beset by slipouts. The trail passes through second-growth forest, dropping into a salmonberry-filled side canyon and then rising on switchbacks to a junction with the Saddler Skyline Trail. Turn left here onto the Skyline route, crossing a creek canyon and then taking switchbacks uphill through more second growth. A series of cathedral tree groupings commences at 1.5 miles as the trail levels. The route then drops on switchbacks, reaching a junction with the Nature Loop to the left at 1.9 miles. Go right, continuing downhill 100 feet to where you cross the campground road. On the far side, the trail plunges into an alder thicket, meeting the Hobbs, Wall Trail on the left. The canyon to the left served as the route for the sixty-five-degree railed incline, but decades of vegetation have obscured the bed where the tracks ran.

Turn right at the junction, taking switchbacks downhill through mixed forest. Recross the campground road at 2.4 miles, pass over a creek that overflows with sword ferns, and then rejoin the Trestle Trail at 2.85 miles. Go left, dropping to meet a paved campground road. Turn left on the road, passing the campground amphitheater before reaching an intersection at 3.0 miles. Turn left at the intersection, reaching a second intersection in 75 yards. Go straight here, crossing the Mill Creek bridge to regain the trailhead.

JEDEDIAH SMITH REDWOODS STATE PARK

Few redwood parks offer more spectacular scenery than "Jed" Smith, yet few, if any, are more misleadingly named. Jedediah Strong Smith was a fur trapper who explored much of the West from 1822 to 1831. With nineteen other trappers and some three hundred horses and mules, he traveled through the North Coast in 1828 on a round-about route from central California to the Rockies. Smith and his party apparently never set foot in any part of what eventually became the park that bears his name. The closest they came was a short distance downstream from the northern boundary of the park when they crossed what later became known as the Smith River. Smith and his men did spend lots of time struggling through terrain that became another redwood park, but that one, despite his presence, was named Del Norte Coast.

Along with the Smith River, many forested areas claim attention in the park. Among the most notable are the magnificent redwood groves near the mouth of Mill Creek, across the river from the park campground; the great stands of trees near Walker Road, a couple of miles west of the river; and the spectacular streamside scenery along the lower stretches of Mill Creek, where maples big and small turn golden in fall. In fact the park is perhaps at its best in autumn, when bigleaf maple, vine maple, and California hazel all shine like lanterns among the shadows of towering redwoods, creating ribbons of pale yellow light that follow the canyons and gorges as they cut across the forested flats. Yet if you find yourself here in spring or summer, Jed Smith will offer plenty of worthy sights—the wild and scenic river rushing bright blue in the sunlight, the many flowering shrubs that color the stream- and riversides, and the more delicate forest flowers that lay scattered beside the trails.

Jedediah Smith Redwoods State Park was the last of the northern parks to be established. It started with a tiny twenty-acre tract of forest in 1928 and, although it added the spectacular Stout Grove the following year, the park didn't grow much for over a decade. Then, in 1939, the state acquired nearly 7000 acres from the Del

Norte Lumber Company. The cost was only $80,000, but much of the property should never have left government ownership in the first place. In the 1880s a banker from Red Bluff circumvented the land laws of the time by recruiting dozens of bogus "homesteaders," who filed false claims and deeded them over to the banker. For all that, the trees didn't know the difference, and they continued to grow in great profusion no matter who owned them. In one location the redwoods were especially noteworthy: along the lower reaches of Mill Creek, a large tributary of the Smith, state park district superintendent Percy French found what he termed the heaviest stands of timber he'd ever cruised—high praise from a man who knew well the magnificence of other great groves such as the Rockefeller Forest.

The Jed Smith Park of today offers two main access routes. Highway 199, which leaves Highway 101 a mile west of the park boundary and enters the northern section of the park, passes gravel-surfaced Walker Road before crossing the Smith River on the Hiouchi bridge. The highway reaches the Jed Smith Campground and visitor center at 4.9 miles on the right, and Redwood National Park's Hiouchi Information Center at 5.0 miles on the left. At 7.2 miles is a junction with South Fork Road on the right. By taking this road 0.4 mile you reach Douglas Park Drive. A right turn here leads to the northern end of the second park access route, Howland Hill Road.

Campsite, Jedediah Smith Redwoods Campground

The southern portion of Jed Smith park is reached by gravel-surfaced Howland Hill Road, an old-time county wagon road that follows the route of the even older Cold Springs Mountain Trail. To reach Howland Hill Road from Highway 101, turn east on Elk Valley Road in southern Crescent City. Take Elk Valley Road 1.1 miles and turn right onto Howland Hill Road. Mileages for trailheads along the road are given from this point. (Mileages from the northern end of the road—starting at the park boundary, where it changes its name from Douglas Park Drive—are then given in parentheses.)

58. BOY SCOUT TREE

Features	▪ long stretches of magnificent, remote redwood forest, the very big Boy Scout Tree, and a small, sparkling waterfall
Distance	▪ 5.6 miles round trip
Elevation gain	▪ 200 feet
Difficulty	▪ strenuous
Open	▪ all year

Driving directions: Drive to mile 3.7 (3.4) of Howland Hill Road. The trailhead is on the north side of the road.

Between Howland Hill Road and Highway 199 lies a vast, roadless redwood forest that forms the heart of Jedediah Smith Redwoods State Park. This hike traverses the southwestern corner of this wilderness, passing through silent stands of ancient trees that seem to have reposed undisturbed for centuries. Every pace you take along the trail takes you farther into the past, into a time when plants, not people, predominated, and when everything was held by the gentle power of the good green earth.

The trailhead is shaded by a mixed forest that features the two largest conifer species in the world. One, of course, is coast redwood. The other—did you guess?—is Douglas-fir.

If Douglas-fir (*Pseudotsuga menziesii*) were a person seeking fame and glory, it would have two reasons to complain. First, it has a problem with its identity: its

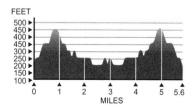

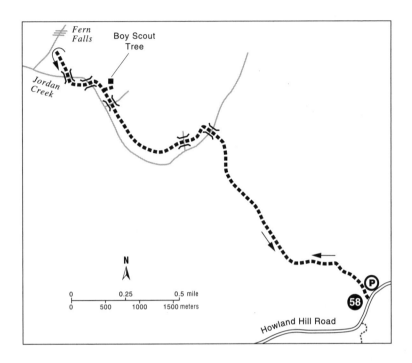

scientific name means "false hemlock," which is why its common name uses a hyphen to indicate that it is not a true fir at all, but part of a separate genera that somewhat resembles both firs and hemlocks. Second, it must stand in the shadow, so to speak, of the coast redwood, which is uniformly acknowledged as being taller. Yet a report from Mineral, Washington, in the foothills of Mount Rainier, told of a Douglas-fir 385 feet tall—taller than any redwood standing today. Unfortunately, the Mineral tree is itself no longer standing, and the current record-holder for the species is a mere 329 feet tall, not enough to raise even an eyebrow in redwood country. Thus it is that the Douglas-fir must look elsewhere for distinctiveness, and a good place to begin is with its cones. True firs all set their cones upright on their limbs, while the Douglas-fir's cones hang below. The cone itself is noteworthy for its "hiding mice," the three-lobed bracts that protrude from beneath the cone scales. The partly obscured bracts resemble nothing so much as the hind legs and tail of a tiny mouse seeking cover beneath the cone scales. It is a charming characteristic that no redwood, regardless of its height, can duplicate.

Tanoak, deer fern, sword fern, and evergreen huckleberry provide a varied understory along the start of the route, which rises intermittently, passing Pacific rhododendron at 0.6 mile. The trail reaches a ridgeline, runs along it for a bit, and drops down the far side through a stand of stately medium-sized redwoods whose trunks rise from the forest floor in seemingly endless profusion.

Steps take you downhill at 1.4 miles to a bridged crossing of Jordan Creek, and more steps then take you up the far side of the canyon. After passing some notably large redwoods, still more steps descend to a side creek and its bridge. The trail undulates along the hillside, Jordan Creek's canyon deepening to the left, and at 1.85 miles a series of big redwoods borders both sides of the path.

The route enters a side canyon where bigleaf and vine maple congregate and crosses another side creek on a railed bridge. Soon the course returns to the main

Boy Scout Tree

canyon. At 2.4 miles an unmarked and poorly maintained side path to the right climbs the hillside to reach the enormous, double-trunked Boy Scout Tree. An aging sign, nailed directly into the bark, provides the designation. Sheriff Jack Breen, who founded the local Boy Scout troop, located the tree many decades ago. The bridge over Mill Creek on Howland Hill Road a short distance north of the trailhead is named for Breen.

Returning to the main trail, you enter an opening in the forest where both coast red elderberry and salmonberry grow beside Jordan Creek. After crossing the stream, you pass bigleaf maple, vine maple, and cascara, and then recross the creek. Use your nose to notice the plants near the bridge, for both stink currant and skunk cabbage grow nearby.

The trail then climbs the hillside before dropping again to end at shaded Fern Falls, which cascades over a rock outcropping bordered by sword fern. Here the route reverses course, reaching the trailhead at 5.6 miles.

59. MILL CREEK SOUTH

Features	■	lovely Mill Creek, colorful bigleaf and vine maples, and massive redwoods and Sitka spruces
Distance	■	1.4 miles round trip (longer option available)
Elevation gain	■	50 feet
Difficulty	■	easy
Open	■	all year

Driving directions: Drive to mile 4.0 (3.1) of Howland Hill Road. The trailhead is on the south side of the road.

From the parking pullout the trail twists through an S-shaped corridor of split-rail fencing, promptly dropping off the benchland to run beside Mill Creek. The rippling waters of the creek reflect the bright hues of California hazel, bigleaf maple, and vine maple, all set against the backdrop of the steep cliff that rises above the far side of the stream. At 0.1 mile a railed bridge crosses a gulch that contains clasping twisted stalk. To the left, masses of lady fern decorate the eastern bank of Mill Creek. The path then switchbacks up the bluff to regain the benchland, moving through a mixed forest of redwood, Douglas-fir, and western hemlock. Soon the route moves away from the main creek, running west along a side canyon, which it crosses at 0.35 mile on a king post bridge. Lady fern and vine maple fill the canyon.

Vine maple (*Acer circinatum*) ranks with poison oak as one of the most colorful plants of the redwood forest. Its nearly circular, multi-lobed leaves glint bright green in spring and summer, while come fall they gradate through various yellows into deep orange and reddish purple, warming the chill creekside air with their brightness. In spring they produce a winged

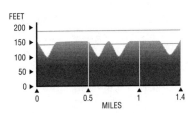

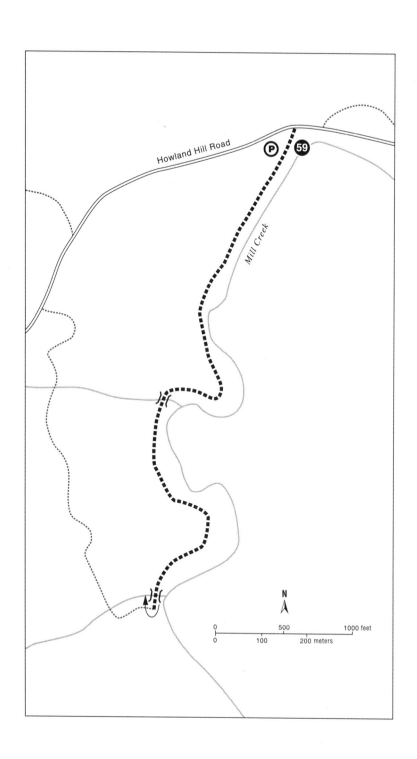

Howland Hill Road

P

59

Mill Creek

N

| 0 | | 500 | | 1000 feet |

| 0 | 100 | | 200 meters |

Kingpost bridge, Mill Creek Trail

fruit, characteristic of maples, called a samara. Its two wings diverge at nearly a 180-degree angle, resembling an airplane propeller. When cast loose from the tree, the samaras twirl groundward in a lazy spiral, softly summoning summer.

Now the trail turns east to again come close above Mill Creek. Vine and bigleaf maples herald a forthcoming section of forest replete with large redwoods and Sitka spruces. The path is bordered by coast boykinia. The trail drops to creekside at 0.55 mile, offering a view of the stream's wide, stone-covered bed before crossing a small side canyon on a second king post bridge. The beauty of the forest rises to a pitch that causes pause: giant Sitka spruces extend skyward like weathered columns, their flaky gray bark in fall offering a harmonious contrast to the masses of yellow and burgundy leaves that adorn the surrounding hazels and maples and that also carpet the forest floor. Here, for a short space, redwoods no longer dominate, and the effect is exhilarating.

All too soon the route concludes at a junction with the Nickerson Trail at mile 0.7. The way left, which once led across Mill Creek to the site of the Nickerson Ranch, is now blocked. The way right heads into heavy forest and reaches Howland Hill Road in a half mile. The Nickerson Trail follows the path of an earlier route, known as the Kelsey Trail, which connected the supply port of Crescent City with the gold mines of the Middle Klamath River. Nickerson's Ranch was itself a mining operation, but neither gold nor any sign of the ranch are now to be found. Kelsey's trail, built in 1855, has been more fortunate; several sections of it are still in service as park or Forest Service routes. However, it would be wise to avoid their higher stretches in winter—a severe storm once caught eighty miners on the trail between Crescent City and Happy Camp, and only after digging for 36 hours through 16 miles of snow did they reach safety.

Mindful of the miners' plight, the hike reverses course at the Nickerson Trail, returning to the trailhead at 1.4 miles.

For a longer hike: Take the Nickerson Trail 0.5 mile to Howland Hill Road. Once there, either double back along the original route for a 2.4-mile total trip, or hike down Howland Hill Road 0.5 mile to the trailhead for a 1.7-mile total trip. Be aware, however, that the road is very dusty during the dry season and that many cars drive by to stir things up.

60. MILL CREEK NORTH

Features	■	a hillside path above lovely Mill Creek, many maples and hazels, and a stunning stand of redwoods
Distance	■	5.7 miles round trip
Elevation gain	■	150 feet
Difficulty	■	strenuous
Open	■	all year

Driving directions: Drive to mile 4.5 (2.6) of Howland Hill Road. The trailhead is on the west side of the road.

In the 1930s, district park superintendent Percy French stated that the lower reaches of Mill Creek contained the heaviest stands of redwoods he had ever cruised. The hike takes you through much of this forest, while also offering you, in fall, glowing glimpses of maple-lined Mill Creek.

You start a short distance south of the Jack Breen Bridge, opposite a small parking area. Another section of the Mill Creek Trail heads south from the parking lot, but your route is westward, across the road, passing between a pair of conifers and entering a leafy wilderness of California hazel, vine maple, red huckleberry, and osoberry. Large redwoods rise above this delicate layer of foliage, while sword ferns spread their fronds like spray from green fountains. Soon the trail climbs the hillside at mile 0.2, offering views of

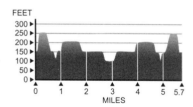

the Jack Breen Bridge and Mill Creek below to the right. A stand of medium-small redwoods is followed by much bigger trees. With their lichen-covered trunks they rise like great gray spires, as if giving shape to the often-present, pervasive mist.

The path switchbacks downhill and levels on a low flat before turning sharply to the right at a huge fallen redwood. Hike next to the log through a corridor composed of overhanging bigleaf maple and vine maple limbs, making a sharp left turn in 50 yards at a break in the log. To the right is a shorter section of another large log, upon which several large roots extend horizontally, resembling the boiler of a steam locomotive.

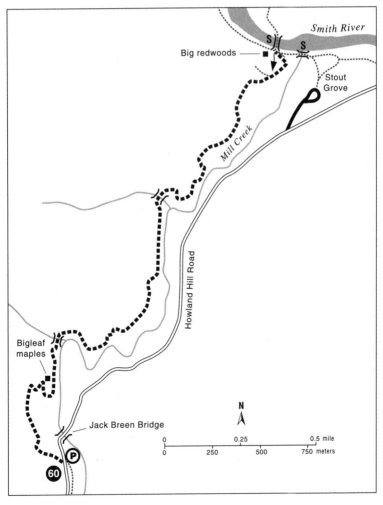

Steps along the Mill Creek Trail

Leaving the logs, you pass a magnificent bigleaf maple on the left at 0.7 mile, with a pair of mossy trunks and a huge arching limb from which lichen hangs like hair from a horse's mane. In fall the maple's golden leaves accentuate the bronze-green hue of the lichen, while underfoot, more leaves lie in an orange-brown carpet, the whole forming a comforting autumn composition.

A switchback then takes the trail to a swalelike flat that sits only a few feet above Mill Creek. Here is a striking view downstream of a boulder-marked bend in the creek. After switchbacking uphill, the route runs across a benchland, crosses a hillside, and enters another benchland. At 1.4 miles a bigleaf maple bends its trunk over the trail into a 180-degree crescent. Soon afterward, Pacific rhododendron, vanilla leaf, and clintonia provide seasonal color. A tiny king post bridge at 1.8 miles spans a rocky cleft in the hillside that sparkles with a small cascade during the wet months. Big redwoods mix with tanoak, western hemlock, and Douglas-fir at 2.3 miles, followed by a thicket of evergreen huckleberry and Pacific rhododendron through which the trail cuts a narrow corridor.

At 2.6 miles go right at a junction with a side trail to the Jensen Grove, continuing on the Mill Creek Trail as it descends to a flat filled with vine maple and California hazel, and, beyond their leafy ribbons, the tall towers of enormous redwoods. The path levels and crosses the edge of the flat. In fall the maples and hazels form a dazzling band of reds and yellows beneath the dark green foliage of the redwoods. After passing through a cathedral cluster of large redwoods, the trail turns away from the edge of Mill Creek to end at a junction with the Hiouchi Trail at 2.85 miles. To the left towers a templelike grove of redwoods, while to the right a path leads to the Hiouchi summer bridge. The route turns back here, returning to the trailhead.

For a longer hike: In season you can turn right at the junction, drop to the banks of the Smith River, and 1) cross the summer bridge to the Jed Smith campground, or 2) continue along the beach to the Mill Creek summer bridge and take the Stout Grove Loop (see Hike 61). Any time of year you can bear left at the junction and follow the Hiouchi Trail (see Hike 62). Taking this latter route for at least a few hundred feet across the magnificent redwood-filled flat is highly recommended.

61. STOUT GROVE LOOP

Features	■	a flat filled with super-sized redwoods, a lovely stream crossing, and glimpses of the Smith River
Distance	■	1.6 miles, loop
Elevation gain	■	100 feet
Difficulty	■	moderate
Open	■	all year

Driving directions: Drive to mile 6.7 (0.4) of Howland Hill Road. Turn north onto the paved access road to the grove parking area.

Drive 0.1 mile to the lot. The trailhead is at the northwestern end of the parking lot loop.

A wide, paved walkway drops past California hazel and bigleaf maple, passing five-finger fern on the bank to the right. Both the grove access road and this first section of trail follow the course of the Cold Springs Mountain Trail, which descended to a crossing of the Smith River just beyond the northern end of the flat. The trail, which was the original route to the gold mines of southern Oregon, was wide enough for wagon travel and had its muddiest sections "corduroyed" with redwood puncheons. The park once maintained a section of the puncheon-covered trail as a hiking route, but it has long been abandoned.

After descending for about 100 yards, the route reaches the Stout Grove, a deeply shaded flat whose main inhabitants are thousands of sword ferns and scores of skyscraping redwoods. A fork at 0.1 mile commences a loop. Turn right, continuing to a junction at 0.25 mile, where you turn right again to follow a side trail that runs above the willow-screened Smith River. A railed bridge at 0.45 mile spans small but picturesque Cedar Creek, its confined canyon filled with the varied foliages of stink currant, vine maple, elk clover, and Pacific rhododendron. The trail then climbs on a set of stairs and undulates across the hillside before ascending on stairs again. Watch for rocks in the intervening trailbed. The path reaches Howland Hill Road at 0.7 mile. Directly across the road is the start of the Little Bald Hills Trail. Turn back here, retracing your steps until you meet the grove loop at mile 1.15. Turn right to continue the loop, enjoying the leafy understory of vine maple and California hazel. After crossing between the root masses of two fallen redwoods, the trail reaches a junction at 1.35 miles. Turn right, passing more large logs, before entering a grove of tall red alder, under which lie a lot of thimbleberry.

Thimbleberry (*Rubus parviflorus*) is an appealing plant, with masses of large, soft green leaves, delicate white flowers, and summer berries that resemble wine-red thimbles. The berries are edible, either cooked or raw, and they can also be made into a liqueur that may bring a flush to one's cheeks. In earlier times the leaves were used for the same effect—pioneer women without access to an Avon representative

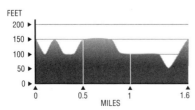

would rub the leaves, which are covered with tiny hairs, against their skin, and presto!—a pleasing blush would result. In fall, those leaves not used for cosmetic purposes create their own coloring, in this case a rich lemon-yellow that brightens the forest wherever they grow.

At 1.45 miles a summer bridge crosses Mill Creek, which empties into the Smith a short distance to your right. Turn around here, reaching the grove loop again, where you bear right. The Stout Tree is now to your left, the largest *sempervirens* in a grove of giants. Its name derives not from its dimension, but from the benefactor whose money purchased the grove, Chicago businessman Frank Deming Stout. A favorite photograph from yesteryear shows a stout President Herbert Hoover joining hands with several associates trying to encircle the tree's tremendous trunk.

At 1.55 miles the trail completes its loop. Turn right and ascend the walkway to the Stout Grove parking lot.

For a longer hike: There are several possibilities: 1) When you reach Howland Hill Road at 0.7 mile, cross the road and take the Little Bald Hills Trail, a route that starts in redwoods but rises to a rocky prairie on the ridgeline. If you turn around at the Little Bald Hills Backcountry Camp, located on the prairie, you add 7 miles to your hike. 2) At the Mill Creek summer bridge, continue across the creek to reach a small beach; here you can cross the Smith River on another summer bridge and reach the Jed Smith Campground. 3) Cross

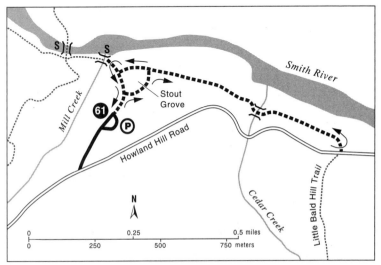

Redwood sorrel

the Mill Creek bridge, hike along the upper side of the beach, and climb the stairs to a trail junction. Turn right and take the Hiouchi Trail (see Hike 62) to the Hiouchi Bridge and back, adding 4 miles to your trip. 4) From the same junction, turn left onto the Mill Creek Trail (see Hike 60), follow it up the canyon of Mill Creek to Howland Hill Road, and then take the road north back to the Stout Grove parking lot. This adds 5.2 miles to your hike.

62. HIOUCHI–SMITH RIVER

Features ▪	the beautiful Smith River and a majestic grove of old-growth redwoods
Distance ▪	4.0 miles round trip
Elevation Change ▪	100 feet
Difficulty ▪	moderate
Open ▪	year round from its northern end; the southern end is most easily reached by summer bridges

Driving directions: Take Highway 199 to a point 4.1 miles east of the Highway 101 interchange, immediately west of the Hiouchi River Bridge. The trailhead is on the southern side of the highway.

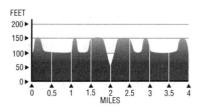

The route starts at a gravel pull-out. A roadbed leads 50 yards to the marked trailhead, which is just to the right of the Hiouchi Bridge. At first you climb the hill, which is shaded by bigleaf maple and red alder. The path levels and then meets the Hatton Trail to the right. Continuing to the left, go downhill through a mixed conifer forest brightened by California hazel. At 0.25 mile the way levels; a spur path to the left leads down to the Smith River and its rocky beach. An opening at 0.4 mile is filled with sun-loving plants, including blueblossom, coastal silk tassel, and ninebark. The trail reenters forest, while the Smith, though obscured by foliage, sings its way down the canyon.

The Smith River, like the adjacent state park, was named for trapper and explorer Jedediah Smith, who, by most accounts, never set foot in what later became the park but did cross the river just downstream in 1828. At the time Smith and nineteen other men were taking a round-about route from central California to a trappers' rendezvous in the Rockies. The trip was more than any of them bargained for. Leading some three hundred horses and pack mules, the party took two months to traverse the mountains separating the Central Valley from the coast, and they then had to work their way through the rugged territory that later became Del Norte Coast Redwoods State Park. Crossing the Smith River was one of the easier parts of the trip. Farther north, at the Umpqua River in southern Oregon, the party was attacked by Indians and only Smith and two others escaped. The men finally reached safety at Fort Vancouver and for a time Smith continued his trapping and exploring. Three years later, however, he encountered his fourth and final Indian attack. Comanches killed Smith near the Arkansas River. Today the Smith River is the last free-flowing river in California, its clear sparkling waters rushing undammed 45 miles from the mountains to the sea. With its restless, unrestrained energy, it recalls the essence of its namesake.

At 0.65 mile the route turns away from the river. Opposite the Treat Grove marker is a colonnade of large redwoods to the left, the nurse log that they sprang from now but a ghost. The path returns to the river, where a railed overlook and bench allow for viewing. Soon the trail is back in forest, rising and then dropping at 1.1 miles past a boulder to the right that is partially covered by licorice fern. After

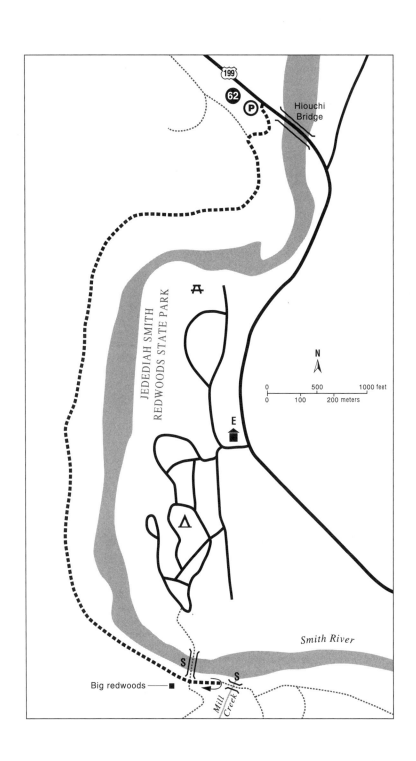

199

62

P

Hiouchi
Bridge

JEDEDIAH SMITH
REDWOODS STATE PARK

N

0   500   1000 feet
0   100   200 meters

E

△

Smith River

S

Big redwoods ──■

S

Mill
Creek

Smith River from Hiouchi Trail

crossing a streamlet the route rises to reach a vista of the Smith and the state park campground on the far bank. A rocky stretch of trail then climbs to another view of the river before reaching a side canyon at 1.6 miles, whose bridge is ornamented by an overhanging vine maple. The path next descends past several boulders, running narrowly across a steep slope. An overlook allows a view upriver of the summer bridge near the mouth of Mill Creek. Presently a wide flat opens to the right. Rising from a covering of sword fern are numerous large redwoods; in the distance a colorful backdrop of vine maples is visible between the dark verticals of the trees' thick trunks. You may feel that you have stumbled upon an ancient temple, the immense columns commanding silence. The distant maples shine through the shadows with a welcoming light.

At the far end of the flat is a junction. The Mill Creek Trail (see Hike 60) branches right, while your route drops left on stairs to a sandy beach. Here a summer bridge to the left crosses to the Jed Smith campground, while the way ahead leads to the Mill Creek summer bridge and the Stout Grove (see Hike 61). Your route stops at the creek, reversing direction to the trailhead at 4.0 miles.

For a longer hike: You can: 1) turn right at the junction with the Mill Creek Trail, hiking it to the Howland Hill Road and back, which will add about 6 miles to your trip; 2) turn left at the Hiouchi summer bridge and cross over to the Jed Smith Campground, where short trails can add variable distances to the hike; 3) cross the Mill Creek summer bridge and hike the Stout Grove Loop, adding 1.8 miles to your trip.

63. SIMPSON-REED AND PETERSON LOOPS

Features	▪	breathtakingly big redwoods and a network of gulches filled with fall-coloring vine maple and California hazel
Distance	▪	0.8 mile double loop
Elevation gain	▪	negligible
Difficulty	▪	easy
Open	▪	all year

Driving Directions: Take Highway 199 to a point 2.9 miles east of the Highway 101 interchange. The trailhead is on the northern side of the road. ***Warning:*** *beware of fast-moving traffic on Highway 199 when turning into or leaving the small parking area.*

These two short loops lie upon a rich benchland, on which several twisting gulches are engraved. Massive redwoods rise from the rich soil, while clusters of deciduous trees wind along the depressions like ribbons decorating the bases of great statues. In fall the hazels and bigleaf maples glow golden, while the vine maples burn like flames of orange and burgundy. The beauty is so captivating that it is easy to wander along the loops with no sense of time or direction, hoping, perhaps to extend the hike and only much later regain the trailhead.

The route begins by a small parking area on the north side of busy Highway 199. A broad path leads into a stand of immense redwoods, dividing in 100 feet. Go straight ahead, ignoring the trail to the left, which marks the end of the hike. This is the Simpson-Reed Loop, named in honor of Mark Reed, the first president of the Simpson Timber Company. Long after Reed's death, Simpson cut voraciously in the Redwood Creek drainage far to the south, perhaps having forgotten the company's earlier history as a protector of redwoods. An opening at 0.05 mile is filled with bushes—coast red elderberry, salmonberry, and both evergreen and red huckleberry.

More large redwoods rise from the forest floor, stretching into the firmament. At 0.2 mile the Peterson Memorial Trail branches right; follow it, crossing a small gulch on a sturdy redwood bridge. Vine maple and California hazel brighten the way. Presently a large bigleaf maple arches its dark trunk over the trail, burrowing its top into the ground so that it is difficult to determine which end is its base. Another stout bridge at 0.35 mile crosses a gulch that overflows with western hemlock, vine maple, and California hazel.

Adding a delicate beauty to the dark and often straight-lined redwood forest, California hazel (*Corylus cornuta* var. *californica*) grows as either a shrub or small tree. It produces an edible nut enclosed in a brown husk shaped like a long-necked flask. The husk has a papery surface, while the leaves, which are usually rounded ovals, are soft and hairy. Soft, too, is their color come fall, when they turn from a

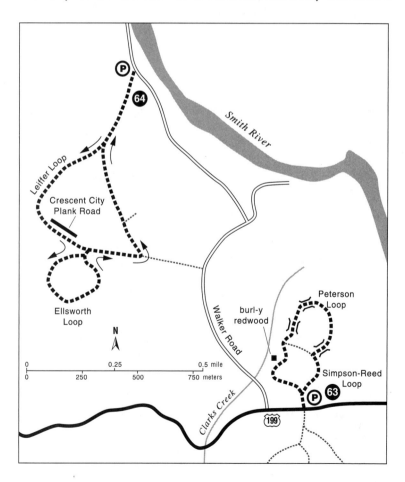

Bigleaf maple leaning over trail

gentle medium green to pale yellow, their leaves a tinted fog hovering above the forest floor.

The large, rock-strewn canyon of Clarks Creek opens to the right of the trail at 0.45 mile. Both maples, vine and bigleaf, rise from the canyon, their leaves filling two levels of the understory. Clintonia and false lily-of-the-valley line the path. Another bridge then spans a side canyon, whereupon the Peterson Loop meets the Simpson-Reed Loop. The route turns right here, moving through more large redwoods. At 0.6 mile an interpretive sign states that "Thick Bark Protects the Redwood from the Flames of Fire." Behind the sign some 50 feet stands a redwood of enormous girth, its base bubbling with burls like the melted wax of a gargantuan candle.

Soon the trail reaches the base of an enormous redwood log; turn left here and follow the log for 100 feet before bearing left and passing numerous vine maples. At 0.75 mile the path passes between the cut sections of a nurse log; western hemlocks grow out of the log on either side. Turn right when you meet the start of the loop trail, which takes you back to the parking area.

64. LEIFFER-ELLSWORTH LOOPS

Features	▪	stately redwoods, a section of nineteenth century wagon road, and many leafy maples
Distance	▪	2.2 miles double loop
Elevation gain	▪	250 feet
Difficulty	▪	moderate
Open	▪	all year

Driving directions: Take Highway 199 to Walker Road, 2.8 miles east of the Highway 101 interchange. Turn north onto gravel-surfaced Walker Road and travel 0.8 mile to a fork. Turn left at the fork and proceed 0.5 mile to a left-hand pullout for the marked trailhead. *Warning: beware of cross traffic on Highway 101 when turning onto Walker Road from the west.*

These charming loops compose the northernmost trails in Redwood National and State Parks. They are also among the nicest to be found in any North Coast parkland. The route here starts from the northern trailhead, which offers a dramatic entrance to the redwood-rich forest.

From the parking area, the trail proceeds southward under a bower of vine maple and California hazel. (See map on page 228.) A patch of salmonberry precedes a row of four large redwoods to the right, which appear to have sprouted centuries ago from a now-vanished nurse log. Other redwoods soon claim attention—some are but scenic snags, others have ornamental burls, while others are simply weathered from great age. Red huckleberry, redwood sorrel, and western burning bush decorate the pathside.

At 0.2 mile the trail divides; this is the start of the Leiffer Loop. Go right, switchbacking past deer fern and salal, passing through a burned-out stump at 0.4 mile. A set of small switchbacks then brings you to the long-abandoned bed of the Crescent City Plank Road. This route, whose name derived from its covering of redwood planks along its muddy stretches, came down the ridge on your right to reach the Smith River, where it crossed at Peacock's Ferry on its way to the Oregon mines. You follow it past clintonia and western trillium, arriving not in Oregon or even at Peacock's Ferry, but at the lip of a

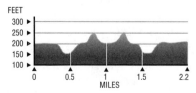

hazel- and maple-filled canyon where the trail takes its own course to reach a junction at 0.8 mile. Turn right, climbing briefly to arrive at the start of the Ellsworth Loop. Turn right again, circling and climbing through hillside redwoods before dropping and completing the circuit at 1.4 miles. A right turn returns you downhill to the Leiffer Loop, where you turn right again to pass beneath vine maple and beside coast boykinia. A row of redwoods to the right completes a stunning sylvan scene.

The hazels continue but now other vivid plants join the mix, which in fall contains all the colors of a traffic signal—the green of California bay, the yellow of bigleaf maple and California hazel, and the red of poison oak. At 1.55 miles you meet a right-hand spur that connects to the southern trailhead. Bypass this short route by turning left, where cascara, thimbleberry, and salmonberry add to the varied collection of leaves. Note the stump on the left at 1.8 miles that bears the indentations of springboard holes. Ignore a short grove trail that branches right and arrive at the end of the Leiffer Loop. A right turn here retraces the spectacular start of the hike to the trailhead.

Deep in the forest on the Ellsworth Loop

APPENDIX I
PARK AND CAMPGROUND INFORMATION

STATE PARK CAMPGROUND RESERVATIONS:
800-444-7275
www.parks.ca.gov
Reservations for all vehicle-accessible camping in the state redwood parks should be made by calling the above number. Reservations must be made at least 48 hours in advance.

Humboldt Redwoods State Park
Box 100
Weott, CA 95571
707-946-2409
hrsp@humboldtredwoods.org
Park headquarters located at Burlington, mile 16.5 (14.5) of the Avenue of the Giants

Humboldt Redwoods Interpretive Association
Box 276
Weott, CA 95571
707-946-2263
vc@humboldtredwoods.org
Park Visitor Center located at Burlington, mile 16.5 (14.5) of the Avenue of the Giants

Campgrounds:
Hidden Springs: located east of Myers Flat at mile 11.5 (19.5) of the Avenue of the Giants; 154 sites, open summer only.
Burlington: located just north of the Visitor Center at mile 16.6 (14.4) of the Avenue of the Giants; 56 sites, open all year.
Albee Creek: located in the Bull Creek Canyon at mile 5.0 of Mattole Road; 34 sites, open summer only.

Other camping: Humboldt Redwoods has walk-in camping at two sites in the Bull Creek Canyon—Baxter Environmental Camp and Hamilton Barn Environmental Camp. It also offers the Williams Grove Group Campground on the Avenue of the Giants and the Cuneo Creek Horse Camp in the Bull Creek Canyon. In addition, the park maintains five backcountry camps in the Bull Creek–Grasshopper Peak backcountry, none of them on the "best short hikes" routes.

Redwood National and State Parks
1111 Second Street
Crescent City, CA 95531
Phone: 707-464-6101
www.nps.gov/redw

Redwood Park Association
Phone: 707-464-9150
www.redwoodparkassociation.org

Crescent City Information Center
1111 Second Street
Crescent City, CA 95531
Phone: 707-464-6101 ext. 5064

Hiouchi Information Center
  Highway 199 (5.0 miles east of
  Highway 101)
  Hiouchi, CA
  Phone: 707-464-6101 ext. 5067
Open summer months

Kuchel Visitor Center
  Highway 101 (1.8 miles south of
  downtown Orick)
  Orick, CA
  Phone: 707-464-6101 ext. 5265

Redwood National Park has no
  vehicle-accessible campgrounds.
  It has backcountry camps at
  Little Bald Hills, Nickel Creek,
  DeMartin (north of Wilson
  Creek), Flint Ridge, Elam, and
  44 Creek. Only the Nickel
  Creek camp is on one of the
  book's hiking routes.

**Prairie Creek Redwoods State
  Park**
  Phone: 707-464-6101 ext. 5301
  Visitor Center located at mile
  1.1 (8.2) of Newton B. Drury
  Scenic Parkway

North Coast Redwood Interpretive
  Association
  Phone: 707-464-6101 ext. 5300
  ncria@carrollsweb.com

Campgrounds:
Elk Prairie: located at mile 1.1 (8.2)
  of Newton B. Drury Scenic
  Parkway; 75 sites, open all year.
Gold Bluffs Beach: located at mile
  5.7 of Davison–Gold Bluffs
  Beach Road; 29 sites, open all
  year.

There are two backcountry camps,
both located along the Gold Bluffs:
Ossagon Creek and Miners Ridge.

**Del Norte Coast Redwoods State
  Park**
There is no park office or visitor
center at Del Norte Coast.
707-464-6101 ext. 5123 for park
ranger.

Campground:
Mill Creek: located at the end of a 2-
mile access road located 7.6 miles
north of the Wilson Creek bridge on
Highway 101; 145 sites, open May 1
to September 30.

**Jedediah Smith Redwoods State
  Park**
  Highway 199 (4.9 miles east of
  Highway 101)
  Hiouchi, CA
  Phone: 707-464-6101 ext. 5113
  Visitor Center, ext. 5112 for
  park ranger: open during
  summer months.

Campground:
Jedediah Smith Campground: located
at the main park entrance on Highway 199, 4.9 miles east of Highway
101; 106 sites, open all year.

APPENDIX II
FURTHER READING

Burt, William H., and Richard P. Grossenheider. *A Field Guide to the Mammals*. Boston and New York: Houghton Mifflin Company, 1980.

Evarts, John, and Marjorie Popper, editors. *Coast Redwood: A Natural and Cultural History*. Los Olivos, CA: Cachuma Press, 2001.

Keator, Glenn. *Pacific Coast Berry Finder*. Berkeley: Nature Study Guild, 1978.

Keator, Glenn, and Ruth M. Heady. *Pacific Coast Fern Finder*. Berkeley: Nature Study Guild, 1981.

Lyons, Kathleen, and Mary Beth Cooney-Lazaneo. *Plants of the Coast Redwood Region*. Boulder Creek, CA: Looking Press, 1988.

Niehaus, Theodore F., and Charles L. Ripper. *A Field Guide to Pacific States Wildflowers*. Boston and New York: Houghton Mifflin Company, 1976.

Peattie, Donald Culross. *A Natural History of Western Trees*. Boston: Houghton Mifflin Company, 1991.

Peterson, Roger Tory. *A Field Guide to Western Birds*. Boston and New York: Houghton Mifflin Company, 1990.

Petrides, George A., and Olivia Petrides. *A Field Guide to Western Trees*. Boston and New York: Houghton Mifflin Company, 1992.

Rohde, Jerry, and Gisela Rohde. *Humboldt Redwoods State Park: The Complete Guide*. Eureka, CA: Miles & Miles, 1992.

Rohde, Jerry, and Gisela Rohde. *Redwood National & State Parks: Tales, Trails, & Auto Tours*. McKinleyville, CA: MountainHome Books, 1994.

Sibley, David Allen. *The Sibley Guide to Birds*. New York: Alfred A. Knopf, 2000.

Stuart, John D., and John O. Sawyer. *Trees and Shrubs of California*. Berkeley, Los Angeles, London: University of California Press, 2001.

There are no detailed, up-to-date maps available for park trails. Both Redwood National and State Parks and Humboldt Redwoods State Park produce maps and guide brochures, available at their visitor centers, that contain general maps of the areas. In addition, Redwood National and State Parks publish an annual "Visitor Guide" with updated information about their parks. USGS maps and map software based on them contain trail information that is badly outdated and should not be relied upon.

INDEX

ABOUT THE AUTHORS

Jerry and Gisela Rohde have written three park guidebooks together, including two for the North Coast redwood parks. They have lived in Humboldt County for over twenty-five years and have hiked the various park trails hundreds of times. They especially enjoy sharing the human and natural history of the area with others.

Photo by Joanna Kalbus

THE MOUNTAINEERS, founded in 1906, is a nonprofit outdoor activity and conservation organization, whose mission is "to explore, study, preserve, and enjoy the natural beauty of the outdoors. . . . " Based in Seattle, Washington, it is now one of the largest such organizations in the United States, with seven branches throughout Washington State.

The Mountaineers sponsors both classes and year-round outdoor activities in the Pacific Northwest, which include hiking, mountain climbing, ski-touring, snowshoeing, bicycling, camping, kayaking, nature study, sailing, and adventure travel. The organization's conservation division supports environmental causes through educational activities, sponsoring legislation, and presenting informational programs.

All its activities are led by skilled, experienced instructors, who are dedicated to promoting safe and responsible enjoyment and preservation of the outdoors.

If you would like to participate in these organized outdoor activities or programs, consider a membership in The Mountaineers. For information and an application, write or call The Mountaineers, 7700 Sand Point Way NE, Seattle, WA 98115; 206-521-6001. You can also visit *www.mountaineers.org* or contact The Mountaineers via email at *info@mountaineers.org*.

The Mountaineers Books, an active, nonprofit publishing program of the organization, produces guidebooks, instructional texts, historical works, natural history guides, and works on environmental conservation. All books produced by The Mountaineers Books fulfill the organization's mission.

The Mountaineers Books
1001 SW Klickitat Way, Suite 201
Seattle, WA 98134
800-553-4453
mbooks@mountaineersbooks.org
www.mountaineersbooks.org

The Mountaineers Books is proud to be a corporate sponsor of The Leave No Trace Center for Outdoor Ethics, whose mission is to promote and inspire responsible outdoor recreation through education, research, and partnerships. The Leave No Trace program is focused specifically on human-powered (nonmotorized) recreation.

Leave No Trace strives to educate visitors about the nature of their recreational impacts, as well as offer techniques to prevent and minimize such impacts. Leave No Trace is best understood as an educational and ethical program, not as a set of rules and regulations.

For more information, visit *www.LNT.org*, or call 800-332-4100.

OTHER TITLES YOU MIGHT ENJOY FROM THE MOUNTAINEERS BOOKS

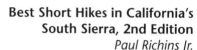

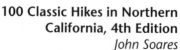
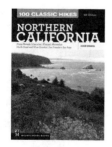